M000107089

**Reproducible Activities**

# Using the Standards
## Measurement

## Grade 3

By
M. J. Owen

**Instructional Fair**
An imprint of Carson-Dellosa Publishing LLC
Greensboro, North Carolina

**Instructional Fair**

Author: M. J. Owen
Editor: Sara Bierling

Instructional Fair
An imprint of Carson-Dellosa Publishing LLC
PO Box 35665
Greensboro, NC 27425 USA

© 2005, Carson-Dellosa Publishing LLC. The purchase of this material entitles the buyer to reproduce worksheets and activities for classroom use only—not for commercial resale. Reproduction of these materials for an entire school or district is prohibited. No part of this book may be reproduced (except as noted above), stored in a retrieval system, or transmitted in any form or by any means (mechanically, electronically, recording, etc.) without the prior written consent of Carson-Dellosa Publishing LLC. Instructional Fair is an imprint of Carson-Dellosa Publishing LLC.

Printed in the USA • All rights reserved.
5 6 7 8 PAH 13 12 11 10

ISBN 978-0-7424-2893-5
202108091

# Table of Contents

# Introduction

This book is designed around the standards from the National Council of Teachers of Mathematics (NCTM), with a focus on measurement. Students will build new mathematical knowledge, solve problems in context, apply and adapt appropriate strategies, and reflect on processes.

The NCTM process standards are also incorporated throughout the activities. The correlation chart on page 6 identifies the pages on which each NCTM measurement substandard appears. Also look for the following process icons on each page.

 Problem Solving           Communication           Reasoning and Proof

 Connections           Representation

**Workbook Pages:** These activities can be done independently, in pairs, or in groups. The problems are designed to stimulate higher-level thinking skills and address a variety of learning styles.

Problems may be broken into parts, with class discussion following student work. At times solution methods or representations are suggested in the activities. Students may gravitate toward using these strategies, but they should also be encouraged to create and share their own strategies.

Many activities will lead into subjects that could be investigated or discussed further as a class. You may want to compare different solution methods or discuss how to select a valid solution method for a particular problem.

**Communication:** Most activities have a communication section. These questions may be used as journal prompts, writing activities, or discussion prompts. Each communication question is labeled **THINK** or **DO MORE**.

© Carson-Dellosa

# Introduction (cont.)

**Create Your Own Problems:** These pages prompt students to create problems like those they completed on the worksheet pages. Encourage students to be creative and to use their everyday experiences. The students' responses will help you to assess their practical knowledge of the topic.

**Check Your Skills:** These activities provide a representative sample of the types of problems developed throughout each section. These can be used as additional practice or as assessment tools.

**Reproducible Rulers:** An inch ruler and a centimeter ruler are provided on page 120 for your convenience.

**Vocabulary Cards:** Use the vocabulary cards to familiarize students with mathematical language. The pages may be copied, cut, and pasted onto index cards. Paste the front and back on the same index card to make flash cards, or paste each side on separate cards to use in matching games or activities.

**Assessment:** Assessment is an integral part of the learning process and can include observations, conversations, interviews, interactive journals, writing prompts, and independent quizzes or tests. Classroom discussions help students learn the difference between poor, good, and excellent responses. Scoring guides can help analyze students' responses. The following is a possible list of problem-solving steps. Modify this list as necessary to fit specific problems.

**1**—Student understands the problem and knows what he is being asked to find.

**2**—Student selects an appropriate strategy or process to solve the problem.

**3**—Student is able to model the problem with appropriate manipulatives, graphs, tables, pictures, or computations.

**4**—Student is able to clearly explain or demonstrate his thinking and reasoning.

© Carson-Dellosa

# NCTM Standards Correlation Chart

| | | Problem Solving | Reasoning and Proof | Communication | Connections | Representation |
|---|---|---|---|---|---|---|
| **Processes** | understand attributes and select units | 10, 28 | 9 | 47 | 29, 39 | 33, 34, 38 |
| | standard units | | 11, 20, 31 | 12, 13 | 14, 30, 35, 36 | 15 |
| | simple unit conversions | 52, 53, 54 | | | 37, 45 | 48, 49, 50, 51 |
| | precision | 19 | 16, 17, 18 | | 21, 22, 46 | 32 |
| | how changing a shape affects measurements | 23, 27 | 24, 42 | | 26, 40, 41 | 25, 43, 44 |
| **Techniques & Tools** | estimate with irregular shapes | 61, 70 | 71, 75 | | 76 | 62, 92 |
| | select and apply appropriate units and tools | 87, 90 | 77 | 91 | 89, 93 | 86, 88 |
| | benchmarks and estimation | 67 | 63, 68 | 94 | 64, 69 | 65 |
| | formulas | 66, 79, 96 | 72, 78, 81 | 83 | 82 | 80, 95 |
| | surface area and volume | 85 | 73, 74, 84 | 100, 101 | 99 | 97, 98 |

The pretest, post test, Create Your Own Problems, and Check Your Skills pages are not included on this chart, but contain a representative sampling of the process standards. Many pages also contain THINK or DO MORE sections, which encourage students to communicate about what they have learned.

© Carson-Dellosa

0-7424-2893-1 • Using the Standards–Measurement 3

# Pretest

Name _____ Date _____

**1.** Which unit is the best to measure the weight of a horse?

    a. gram         b. cup         c. pound         d. inch

**2.** Which formula would be best to find the area of a square?

    a. width x width     b. length x width     c. length + width   d. area x volume

**3.** Which unit is not used to measure weight?

    a. gram         b. mile         c. kilogram         d. ounce

**4.** About how many inches are in 10 centimeters?

    a. 12         b. 8         c. 6         d. 4

**5.** About how many ounces are in 4 pounds?

    a. 48         b. 64         c. 18         d. 24

**6.** What is the perimeter of the rectangle?

8 inches

5 inches                             5 inches

8 inches

    a. 16 inches     b. 18 inches     c. 22 inches     d. 26 inches

7

© Carson-Dellosa                   0-7424-2893-1 • Using the Standards–Measurement 3

Name _____  Date _____

# Pretest (cont.)

**7.** Circle the square that has the greatest number of square units.

a. 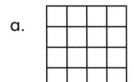  b.  c. 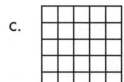  d.

**8.** It is a sunny day. The temperature is 78° Fahrenheit. Which thermometer shows this temperature?

a. 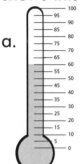  b. 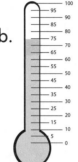  c. 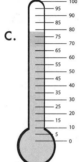  d.

**9.** The scale on a map shows that 1 inch equals 10 miles. If the store is 3 inches from the library, how many miles is the store from the library?

a. 3 miles          b. 30 miles          c. 13 miles          d. 10 miles

**10.** How many inches are in 3 feet?

a. 12          b. 24          c. 36          d. 18

**11.** About how much water does a bathtub hold?

a. 40 cups          b. 40 pints          c. 40 gallons          d. 40 yards

**12.** Which object is the heaviest?

a. shoe          b. coat          c. mittens          d. box of tissues

© Carson-Dellosa          0-7424-2893-1 • Using the Standards–Measurement 3

Name _____ Date _____

# Estimate the Length

Look at each of the following six items in your classroom. First estimate the length of each object. Write your estimate in the chart. Then find the actual length. Write the actual length in the chart. Was your estimate close to the actual measurement?

| Item | Estimate | Actual |
|------|----------|--------|
| **1.** length of a stapler | | |
| **2.** length of the chalkboard | | |
| **3.** length of a small table | | |
| **4.** length of the teacher | | |
| **5.** width of a desk | | |
| **6.** width of the classroom door | | |

## THINK

Were the estimates close to the actual measurements? Why do you think the estimates may have been closer for some objects than others?

© Carson-Dellosa    0-7424-2893-1 • Using the Standards–Measurement 3

# Choose the Best Unit

Think about the length of each object. Then choose the best unit of measurement for each.

1. length of baseball bat
   a. inch
   b. foot
   c. yard
   d. centimeter

2. height of a box of cookies
   a. mile
   b. foot
   c. yard
   d. centimeter

3. length of a crocodile
   a. inch
   b. foot
   c. yard
   d. centimeter

4. length of a bug
   a. milliliter
   b. foot
   c. yard
   d. centimeter

5. height of a stop sign
   a. inch
   b. foot
   c. yard
   d. centimeter

6. length of a piece of chalk
   a. inch
   b. foot
   c. yard
   d. centimeter

Write the best unit of measurement for each.

7. length of a table _____

8. width of a school gym _____

## DO MORE

Choose three other items from your classroom. Use a ruler or measuring tape to measure each one. Write the objects in order from longest to shortest.

10

# Is It Close?

Use a ruler. Find one item that measures close to each of the following lengths. Write the name of each object on the line.

**1.**   6 inches _____

**2.**   4 inches _____

**3.**   $10\frac{1}{2}$ inches _____

Use a tape measure. Find one item that measures close to each of the following lengths. Write the name of each object on the line.

**4.**   3 feet_____

**5.**   $5\frac{1}{2}$ feet_____

**6.**   8 feet_____

Use a yard stick. Find one item that measures close to each of the following lengths. Write the name of each object on the line.

**7.**   2 yards _____

**8.**   $4\frac{1}{2}$ yards _____

**9.**   1 yard _____

## DO MORE

Use a ruler, tape measure, or yardstick to measure the length of three items that you use when you are getting ready for school. List the items in order from shortest to longest.

**11**

Name _____ Date _____

# What Is a Foot?

You decide to use the length of your foot as a tool for measuring different items around your room. Use the Venn diagram below to compare your foot as a measuring tool to a foot-long ruler.

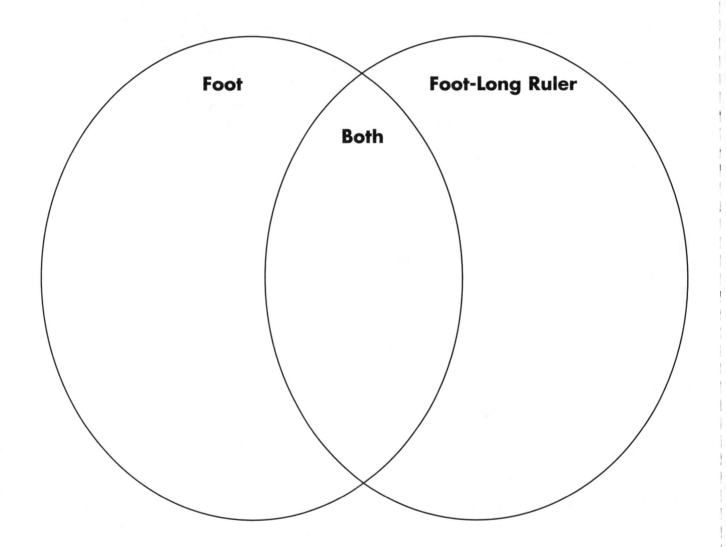

**Foot**

**Foot-Long Ruler**

**Both**

## DO MORE

Read the picture book *How Big Is a Foot?* by Rolf Myller to yourself or with a friend. Write between one and two paragraphs explaining what you learned about nonstandard units from reading this book.

© Carson-Dellosa

Name _____ Date _____

# Use Your Foot

Trace your foot in the space below.

Is your foot bigger or smaller than a standard foot? By how much?

_____

© Carson-Dellosa    0-7424-2893-1 • Using the Standards–Measurement 3

Name _____ Date _____

# *Linear Measurement*

Fill in each answer choice with one of the following standard units of measurement: *inch, foot, yard,* or *mile.*

1. The teacher's pen is about $6\frac{1}{2}$ _____ long.

2. It takes Tom about 30 minutes to walk to school. He lives about 2 _____ from school.

3. The baseball bat is about 3 _____ long.

4. The football is about 8 _____ long.

5. Yolanda runs about 100 _____ between two goal posts on a soccer field.

6. Ms. Clark jogs 3 _____ every morning before school.

7. Wesley is the tallest boy on his basketball team. He is 6 _____ tall.

8. It takes Betty's mom about 3 _____ of fabric to make a new dress.

9. The school bus is about 18 _____ long.

10. Joy's telephone cord is about 8 _____ in length.

## DO MORE

Write two more fill-in-the-blank measurement problems. Challenge a classmate to solve them.

© Carson-Dellosa  0-7424-2893-1 • Using the Standards–Measurement 3

Name _____ Date _____

# *Metric Length*

Use a centimeter ruler. Find one item that measures close to each of the following lengths. Write the name of each object on the line.

**1.** 6 centimeters _____

**2.** $8\frac{1}{2}$ centimeters _____

**3.** 9 centimeters _____

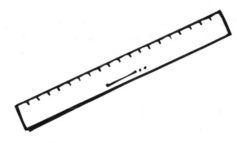

Use a meter stick. Find one item that measures close to each of the following lengths. Write the name of each object on the line.

**4.** 1 meter _____

**5.** $5\frac{1}{2}$ meters _____

**6.** 6 meters _____

**7.** $3\frac{1}{2}$ meters _____

**8.** 2 meters _____

## DO MORE

Use a centimeter ruler or meter stick to measure the length of three items that you use at school. List the items in order from shortest to longest.

© Carson-Dellosa  0-7424-2893-1 • Using the Standards–Measurement 3

Name _____ Date _____

# Pencil Length

Use a ruler to measure each pencil in inches.

**1.**

**2.**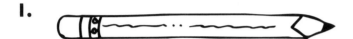

**3.**

**4.**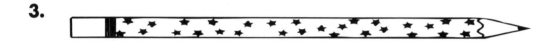

**5.**

**6.**

**7.**

**8.**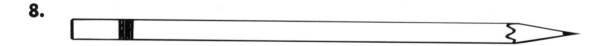

**THINK**

Number the pencils from 1–8, according to length. The shortest pencil is #1.

© Carson-Dellosa                    0-7424-2893-1 • Using the Standards–Measurement 3

# *Draw It*

Use your ruler to draw lines the following lengths.

**1.** Draw a line $3\frac{1}{2}$ centimeters long.

**2.** Draw a line 4 centimeters long.

**3.** Draw a line 6 centimeters long.

**4.** Draw a line $8\frac{1}{2}$ centimeters long.

**5.** Draw a line 7 centimeters long.

**6.** Draw a line $9\frac{1}{2}$ centimeters long.

**THINK**

 About how many centimeters are in 1 inch?

© Carson-Dellosa 0-7424-2893-1 • Using the Standards–Measurement 3

# Longer Than a Foot

Use a yardstick to measure the following items.

**1.** length of your classroom door _____

**2.** width of your classroom door _____

**3.** width of your desk_____

**4.** distance between your desktop and the floor_____

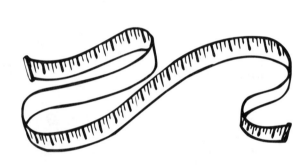

Use a tape measure to find items that are about the following lengths.

**5.** 6 feet_____

**6.** $9\frac{1}{2}$ feet_____

**7.** 3 feet_____

**8.** $12\frac{1}{2}$ feet _____

## THINK

Measurement is important in many occupations. Think of one occupation where you might be likely to use measurement skills. Write about how you might use measurement in this occupation.

18

Name _____ Date _____

# *Playground Measuring*

Use a tape measure to measure the following items.

**1.** length of a slide _____

**2.** height of the swing seats from the ground _____

**3.** length of a picnic table _____

**4.** width of a picnic table _____

**5.** length of the monkey bars _____

Look around outside. Find items that measure about the following lengths.

**6.** $4\frac{1}{2}$ feet _____

**7.** 8 feet _____

**8.** $2\frac{1}{2}$ feet _____

## THINK

About how tall should the monkey bars be so that students don't hit their heads when hanging upside down?

**19**

# *String Length*

You need string and scissors.

Cut string to the following lengths. Then arrange the strings in order from shortest to longest.

**Inches:**   3 inches   $2\frac{1}{2}$ inches   5 inches

$8\frac{1}{2}$ inches   10 inches

**Centimeters:**   6 centimeters   12 centimeters   $5\frac{1}{2}$ centimeters

9 centimeters   $10\frac{1}{2}$ centimeters

Compare the $2\frac{1}{2}$-inch string to the 6-centimeter string.

_____

_____

_____

_____

_____

**DO MORE**

 Make a design using some of the strings that you have cut. Measure the lengths of the sides of your design.

© Carson-Dellosa

Name _____ Date _____

# *Estimate and Actual*

Estimate the length of each object. Then measure each item. Write the actual measurement on the line provided.

|     |                                          | **Estimate** | **Actual** |
|-----|------------------------------------------|--------------|------------|
| 1.  | length of your classroom                 | _____    | _____  |
| 2.  | width of your classroom                  | _____    | _____  |
| 3.  | width of the board in your classroom     | _____    | _____  |
| 4.  | length of your pencil box                | _____    | _____  |
| 5.  | length of your book bag                  | _____    | _____  |
| 6.  | length of one of your textbooks          | _____    | _____  |
| 7.  | length of your eraser                    | _____    | _____  |
| 8.  | length of one bookshelf in your classroom| _____    | _____  |

## DO MORE

Find the difference between each of your estimates and each actual answer.

© Carson-Dellosa          0-7424-2893-1 • Using the Standards–Measurement 3

Name _____ Date _____

# City Distance

Write the name of your city on the line. _____

List five cities or towns that are close to where you live. Beside the name of each town, estimate the distance between your city and that city.

1. _____ _____

2. _____ _____

3. _____ _____

4. _____ _____

5. _____ _____

Find a map or use the Internet to find the actual distance between your city and each city that you listed.

1. _____

2. _____

3. _____

4. _____

5. _____

## DO MORE

Pretend you are able to drive 60 miles in 1 hour. Based on this information, how long would it take you to travel between your city and each of the cities that you listed?

© Carson-Dellosa    0-7424-2893-1 • Using the Standards–Measurement 3

Name _____ Date _____

# Shape Perimeter

Find the perimeter of each shape.

**1.**

2 cm    $3\frac{1}{2}$ cm

2 cm

**2.**

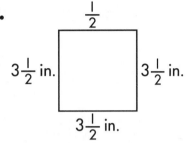

$\frac{1}{2}$

$3\frac{1}{2}$ in.    $3\frac{1}{2}$ in.

$3\frac{1}{2}$ in.

**3.**

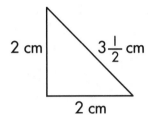

3 cm

$1\frac{1}{2}$ cm    $1\frac{1}{2}$ cm

**4.**

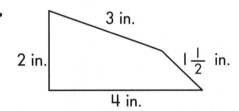

3 in.

2 in.    $1\frac{1}{2}$ in.

4 in.

**5.**

2 in.

$4\frac{1}{2}$ in.    $4\frac{1}{2}$ in.

3 in.

**6.**

$8\frac{1}{2}$ in.

$8\frac{1}{2}$ in.    $8\frac{1}{2}$ in.

$8\frac{1}{2}$ in.

**7.**

$7\frac{1}{2}$ cm

$7\frac{1}{2}$ cm

**8.**

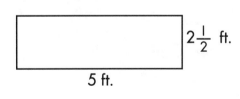

$2\frac{1}{2}$ ft.

5 ft.

## DO MORE

Write down the length of each side of your classroom. What is the perimeter of your classroom?

**23**

# Create Shapes

Draw shapes with each of the side lengths provided.

**1.**  $1\frac{1}{2}$ cm, 2 cm, $1\frac{1}{2}$ cm

**2.**  four sides $4\frac{1}{2}$ cm

**3.**  two sides $3\frac{1}{2}$ cm, two sides 4 cm

**4.**  $6\frac{1}{2}$ cm, 5 cm, 4 cm, $3\frac{1}{2}$ cm, $6\frac{1}{2}$ cm

**5.**  six sides 7 cm

## THINK

Think of three real-life situations when you might need to find perimeter. Write about each situation.

**24**

Name _____ Date _____

# *The Size of Shapes*

**1.** Draw a pentagon with each side measuring $3\frac{1}{2}$ centimeters.

**2.** Draw an octagon with each side measuring $8\frac{1}{2}$ centimeters.

**3.** Draw an equilateral triangle with each side measuring $1\frac{1}{2}$ inches.

**4.** Draw a hexagon with each side measuring $5\frac{1}{2}$ centimeters.

**5.** Draw a shape that has a perimeter of 10 centimeters.

**THINK**

Marcy is building a fence around her square yard. Each side of her yard measures 10 feet. It will take her about three hours to build each 10-foot section of fence. About how long will it take Marcy to build her fence?

25

Name _____ Date _____

# Measurement Word Problems

Solve the following perimeter word problems.

1. Kelsey has a square pool. Each side of her pool measures 150 feet in length. Every morning she swims ten lengths in her swimming pool. How many feet does she swim each morning?

2. A carpenter charges $10.00 for each foot in height of a bookshelf that he designs and builds. He builds a bookshelf that is 8 feet high and 6 feet wide. How much does he charge for the bookshelf?

3. Jamal wants to fence a rectangular space that is 150 feet by 200 feet. What is the perimeter of the space that Jamal wants to fence in?

4. Each side of Mia's room is 10 feet. She hangs a picture every 4 feet in her room. How many pictures does Mia hang in her room in all?

5. Keisha is making a picture frame for her painting. Each side of her square picture frame is 36 inches. What is the perimeter in feet of the picture frame that Keisha makes?

## DO MORE

Write your own perimeter word problem. Challenge a classmate to solve it.

© Carson-Dellosa

Name _____ Date _____

# *Classroom Perimeter*

Find the perimeter of each of the following objects.

**1.** textbook _____

**2.** book you are reading _____

**3.** your desk _____

**4.** room in your school _____

**5.** table _____

**6.** your lunchbox _____

**7.** school lunch tray _____

**8.** List the items above from least to greatest according to each item's perimeter. Use the problem numbers to list them.

_____

_____

_____

**DO MORE**

Measure the table in millimeters. Compare answers with classmates. Did you get the same answer? Then measure the table in inches. Did you get the same answer?

© Carson-Dellosa 0-7424-2893-1 • Using the Standards–Measurement 3

Name _____    Date _____

# *Estimating Weight*

Look at each object. Circle the best estimate for the weight of each item.

**1.**

    a. 60 ounces
    b. 6 pounds
    c. 6 kilograms
    d. 28 grams

**2.**

    a. 11 ounces
    b. $1\frac{1}{2}$ pounds
    c. 100 kilograms
    d. 10 inches

**3.**

    a. 3 ounces
    b. 4 pounds
    c. 14 kilograms
    d. 4 yards

**4.**

    a. 12 ounces
    b. 22 pounds
    c. 121 kilograms
    d. 12 grams

**5.**

    a. 4 milliliters
    b. 4 pounds
    c. 4 centimeters
    d. 4 ounces

**6.**

    a. 16 ounces
    b. 30 pounds
    c. 6 kilograms
    d. 64 liters

## DO MORE

 What are your favorite animals? First make a list of your four favorite animals. Then use an encyclopedia or the Internet to find their weights. Write the animals' names in order from least to greatest based on weight.

© Carson-Dellosa    0-7424-2893-1 • Using the Standards–Measurement 3

Processes

Name _____   Date _____

# *Matching Weights*

Cut out the five objects. Look at the weights listed below. Glue each object above the best estimate of its weight.

**1.**

6 ounces

**2.**

42 pounds

**3.**

170 ounces

**4.**

12 pounds

**5.**

90 ounces

  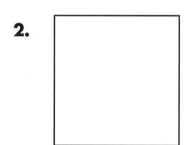  

29

© Carson-Dellosa

0-7424-2893-1 • Using the Standards–Measurement 3

Name _____ Date _____

# Ounces and Pounds

Fill in each answer choice with one of the following standard units of measurement: *ounces* or *pounds*.

**1.** A baseball might weigh about 6 _____.

**2.** Sara's dog loves to go running with her. Her dog weighs about 60 _____.

**3.** Maria's mom weighs about 140 _____.

**4.** Tina's shoelaces weigh about 1 _____.

**5.** Manolo's cell phone weighs about 10 _____.

**6.** Draw a picture of something that you think might weigh about 25 pounds.

**7.** Draw a picture of something that you think might weigh about 50 pounds.

**8.** Draw a picture of something that you think might weigh about 5 pounds.

**30**

© Carson-Dellosa

Name _____ Date _____

# Grams and Kilograms

Weigh each of the following five items on a scale. Write the weight of each item using *grams* or *kilograms*.

**1.** sheet of notebook paper_____

**2.** folder _____

**3.** textbook _____

**4.** 3 pencils_____

**5.** 10 paper clips _____

**6.** Now write the names of the items that you weighed in order from least to greatest on the lines.

_____

_____

Weigh each of the following items on a scale. Write the weight of each item on the line using pounds.

**7.** 3 textbooks_____

**8.** 1 small chair _____

**9.** you _____

## DO MORE

Find out how much you weighed when you were born. How much do you weigh now? How much more do you weigh now than when you were born?

**31**

Name _____ Date _____

# *Pounds of Apples*

Marissa buys apples at the store. Read each scale. Record the weight of apples shown on each scale. Then rank the scales in order from least to greatest.

**1.**

_____

_____

**2.**

_____

_____

**3.**

_____

_____

**4.**

_____

_____

**5.**

_____

_____

**6.**

_____

_____

## DO MORE

Visit a grocery store. Weigh 2 apples, 4 apples, and 6 apples separately. Based on this information, about how much do you think 1 apple weighs?

© Carson-Dellosa

0-7424-2893-1 • Using the Standards–Measurement 3

Name _____ Date _____

# Prism Volume

Find the volume of each prism.

**1.** 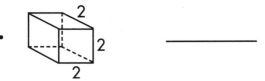 _____

**2.** 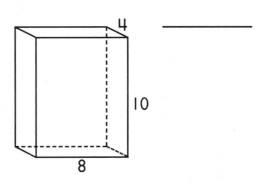 _____

**3.** 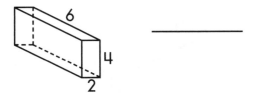 _____

**4.** 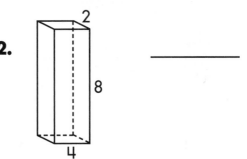 _____

**5.** _____

Use the information to find the volume of each rectangular prism described below.

**6.** length = 4, width = 2, height = 1 _____

**7.** length = 5, width = 4, height = 2 _____

**8.** length = 6, width = 3, height = 5 _____

**9.** length = 2, width = 4, height = 2 _____

**10.** length = 6, width = 6, height = 1 _____

## DO MORE

Make five different shapes using connecting cubes. Find the volume of each shape that you create. Line the shapes up in order of least to greatest volume.

**33**

Name _____ Date _____

# Find the Volume

Find the volume of each shape.

**1.** 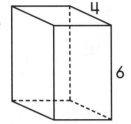   _____

**2.** 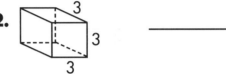   _____

**3.** _____

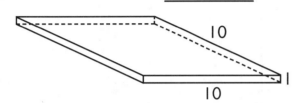

**4.** 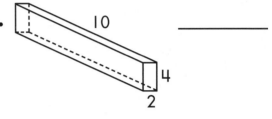   _____

**5.**

_____

Draw each shape using each of the following descriptions.

**6.** Draw a cube that has a length of 2 inches, a height of 2 inches, and a width of 2 inches.

**7.** Draw a rectangular prism that has a length of 1 unit, a height of 4 units, and a width of 2 units.

## THINK

 What formula is used to find the volume of a cube? Why do you think the formula works?

**34**

© Carson-Dellosa   0-7424-2893-1 • Using the Standards–Measurement 3

Name _____ Date _____

# *Customary Capacity*

Fill in each answer choice with one of the following standard units of measurement: *cup*, *quart*, or *gallon*.

**1.** Jasmine poured 2 _____ of milk in a small measuring cup to add to the cookies.

**2.** My bathtub holds about 40 _____ of water.

**3.** Terri purchases the largest container of milk at the grocery store. She purchases a 1 _____ container.

**4.** Matt drinks a box of apple juice with his lunch. His box of apple juice contains about 1 _____ of juice.

Match each picture to the correct word.

**5.**                                               quart

**6.**                                               gallon

**7.**                                               pint

**8.**                                               cup

## DO MORE

  Visit your local grocery store. Find three different types of liquid you would like to buy. List each item and the unit that is used to measure it.

© Carson-Dellosa                                    0-7424-2893-1 • Using the Standards–Measurement 3

Name _____ Date _____

# Metric Capacity

Read each sentence. Write *milliliter(s)* or *liter(s)* on the line.

1. Peter rinses his mouth with about 25 _____ of water when he brushes his teeth.

2. Davor drinks a large cup of orange juice with breakfast. He drinks about 100 _____ of orange juice.

3. Teo's aquarium needs to be refilled. He refills it with about 50 _____ of water.

4. Ursula's swimming pool is filled with about 250,000 _____ of water.

Read each sentence. Write *gram(s)* or *kilogram(s)* on the line.

5. Marta gathers 6 paper clips for her report. They weigh a total of about 6 _____.

6. Mateo loads 2 bicycles on the front of the bus. The 2 bikes weigh about 70 _____.

7. The thumb tack Becky finds on the floor weighs about 1 _____.

8. While Mr. Cohen works out he carries weights weighing about 3 _____.

## DO MORE

Use a scale to find the weight in pounds or kilograms of at least five items around your classroom.

© Carson-Dellosa 0-7424-2893-1 • Using the Standards–Measurement 3

# Comparing Capacity

Look at the information in the box. Then complete the equations.

| 2 cups = 1 pint | 1 quart = 4 cups | 1 gallon = 4 quarts |
|---|---|---|

**1.** 3 pints = _____ cups

**2.** 2 quarts = _____ cups

**3.** 2 gallons = _____ quarts

**4.** 24 quarts = _____ gallons

**5.** 8 pints = _____ cups

**6.** 6 quarts = _____ cups

**7.** 12 cups = _____ pints

**8.** 5 quarts = _____ pints

**9.** 8 cups = _____ quarts

**10.** 6 gallons = _____ quarts

## DO MORE

Find a recipe. Double the recipe and convert units when necessary.

© Carson-Dellosa

0-7424-2893-1 • Using the Standards–Measurement 3

Name _____ Date _____

# Find the Area

Find the area of each shape.

**1.**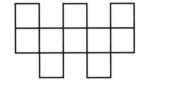

_____

**2.**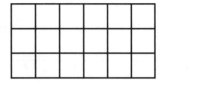

_____

**3.**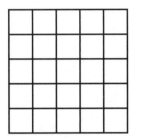

_____

**4.**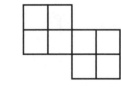

_____

**5.**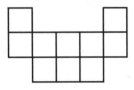

_____

**6.**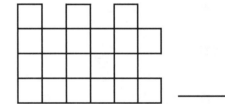

_____

**7.**

_____

**8.**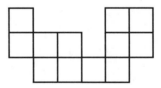

_____

## DO MORE

Make a shape on a piece of 1-in. graph paper. Color in your shape. Then find the area of your shape.

© Carson-Dellosa   0-7424-2893-1 • Using the Standards–Measurement 3

Name _____ Date _____

# *Shape Area*

Create each shape. Try to use all stright lines. Then find the area of the shape you drew.

**I.**　　house

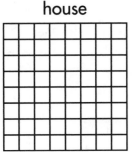

What is the area of the house? _____

**2.**　　gift

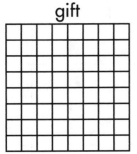

What is the area of the gift? _____

**3.**　　animal

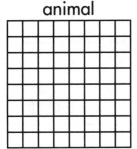

What is the area of the animal? _____

## DO MORE

What other animals do you think you could draw on graph paper? Draw another animal on a piece of graph paper. What is the area of the animal?

© Carson-Dellosa　　　0-7424-2893-1 • Using the Standards–Measurement 3

Name _____ Date _____

# *Bedroom Map*

**1.** Krista wants to put a desk in her room. The area of the desk is 10 square units. Draw the desk on the room grid below. Make sure it is by a window. Krista likes to look outside when she writes.

**2.** Krista's clothes are falling out of her closet. She needs to buy a dresser. She finds a used one that takes up 12 square units of floor space. Draw a dresser on the room grid below.

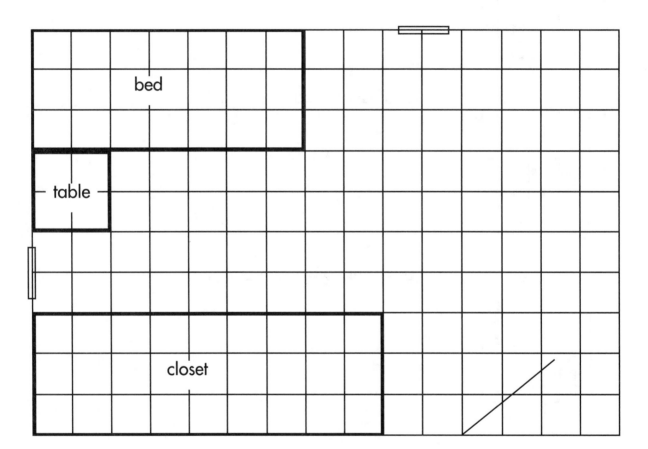

© Carson-Dellosa

0-7424-2893-1 • Using the Standards–Measurement 3

Name _____ Date _____

# *Reflecting Area*

Look at each shaded region. Write the area. Then draw a reflection of the shaded shape across the line of symmetry. Write the area of the whole shape.

**1.**

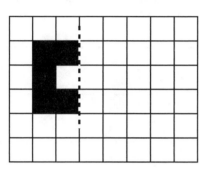

area 1 _____   area 2 _____

**2.**

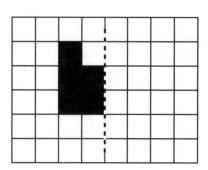

area 1 _____   area 2 _____

**3.**

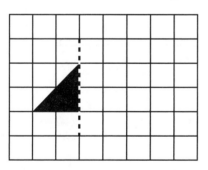

area 1 _____   area 2 _____

**4.**

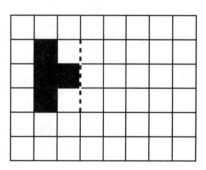

area 1 _____   area 2 _____

## THINK

How does drawing a reflection affect the area and why?

© Carson-Dellosa

0-7424-2893-1 • Using the Standards–Measurement 3

Name _____ Date _____

# Square Units

Find the area of each. Write your answer using square units.

**1.**   length = 5 inches, width = 4 inches _____

**2.**   length = 4 feet, width = 2 feet _____

**3.**   length = 1 inch, width = 4 inches _____

**4.**   length = 10 centimeters, width = 4 centimeters _____

**5.**   length = 3 inches, width = 3 inches _____

**6.**   length = 2 centimeters, width = 5 centimeters _____

**7.**   length = 1 centimeter, width = 1 centimeter _____

**8.**   length = 5 centimeters, width = 7 centimeters _____

**9.**   length = 9 feet, width = 3 feet _____

**10.**   length = 4 inches, width = 9 inches _____

## DO MORE

Trace your hand on a sheet of graph paper. Shade in each box within your outline. What is the approximate area of your hand?

42

Name _____ Date _____

# Matching Area

Match each picture to the answer that represents its area.

**1.**  18 square units

**2.**  22 square units

**3.**  6 square units

**4.**  10 square units

**5.**  20 square units

**6.**  4 square units

**7.**  12 square units

## DO MORE

Draw three different shapes that all have the same area.

© Carson-Dellosa  0-7424-2893-1 • Using the Standards–Measurement 3

Name _____ Date _____

# Create an Area

Draw shapes with the following areas.

**1.** Area = 15 square units

**2.** Area = 8 square units

**3.** Area = 25 square units

**4.** Area = 12 square units

**5.** Area = 18 square units

## DO MORE

On a sheet of graph paper draw as many different rectangles as you can that have an area of 12 square units.

**44**

Name _____  Date _____

# *Workout Time*

Rachel records the amount of time she spends exercising each day. She only records her time in minutes. How many hours did Rachel spend working out during this two-week period? Write two sentences or draw to show how you found your answer.

_____

_____

_____

# February

| Sunday | Monday | Tuesday | Wednesday | Thursday | Friday | Saturday |
|---|---|---|---|---|---|---|
| 1 <br> 65 minutes | 2 <br> 80 minutes | 3 <br> 120 minutes | 4 <br> 75 minutes | 5 <br> 0 minutes | 6 <br> 0 minutes | 7 <br> 90 minutes |
| 8 <br> 90 minutes | 9 <br> 65 minutes | 10 <br> 80 minutes | 11 <br> 120 minutes | 12 <br> 60 minutes | 13 <br> 90 minutes | 14 <br> 75 minutes |
| 15 | 16 | 17 | 18 | 19 | 20 | 21 |
| 22 | 23 | 24 | 25 | 26 | 27 | 28 |

## DO MORE

How much time do you spend sleeping each week? Record the time you go to bed and get up each day. How much time did you sleep during the week?

© Carson-Dellosa  0-7424-2893-1 • Using the Standards–Measurement 3

Name _____ Date _____

# How Long Does It Take?

Estimate the amount of time each of the following activities takes.

1. wake up _____
2. get to school_____
3. go to recess _____
4. eat lunch_____
5. get home from school _____
6. eat dinner_____
7. finish your homework _____
8. spend time with your family _____

Now keep a watch by your side. Find the actual amount of time each of the following activities takes.

1. wake up _____
2. get to school_____
3. go to recess _____
4. eat lunch_____
5. get home from school _____
6. eat dinner_____
7. finish your homework _____
8. spend time with your family _____

## THINK

What is the difference between an estimate and an actual answer? Can you think of a time when an estimate would be a good answer? Can you think of a time that only an exact answer would do?

**46**

Name _____ Date _____

# *Angle Degrees*

Match each angle to its definition.
*Helpful Hint:* Remember, a right angle is 90°.

**1.**

less than a right angle

**2.**

right angle

**3.**

less than a right angle

**4.**

greater than a right angle

greater than a right angle

**5.**

## THINK

What does the ° symbol mean?

**47**

Name _____ Date _____

# Convert the Units

Convert customary units. Write your answers on the lines provided.

1. 36 inches = _____ feet

2. 12 feet = _____ inches

3. 12 inches = _____ feet

4. 48 inches = _____ feet

5. 6 feet = _____ inches

6. 8 quarts = _____ gallons

7. 2 gallons = _____ quarts

8. 16 ounces = _____ pounds

9. 4 pounds = _____ ounces

10. 32 ounces = _____ pounds

Solve the following word problem.

11. Francis is making scarves for his friends for the holidays. He buys 18 yards of fabric. He will need 3 square feet of material for each scarf. How many scarves can Francis make from 18 yards of fabric?

## DO MORE

Write your own word problem that involves converting customary units. Challenge a classmate to solve your problem.

© Carson-Dellosa

0-7424-2893-1 • Using the Standards–Measurement 3

Name _____ Date _____

# *Equivalent Units*

Match each problem to an equal amount by drawing a line.

| | | | | |
|---|---|---|---|---|
| **1.** | 2 pints | a. | 8 quarts | |
| **2.** | 36 inches | b. | 8 cups | |
| **3.** | 32 ounces | c. | 48 inches |  |
| **4.** | 2 gallons | d. | 2 pounds | |
| **5.** | 12 inches | e. | 5 pounds |  |
| **6.** | 4 pints | f. | 4 cups | |
| **7.** | 80 ounces | g. | 3 feet |  |
| **8.** | 4 feet | h. | 1 foot | |

Convert each measurement to an equivalent amount. You choose the unit.

**9.** $2\frac{1}{2}$ cups _____

**10.** 40 gallons _____

**11.** 16 ounces _____

## THINK

Why is it important to be able to convert units of measurement? When would knowing how to convert units of measurement help you?

© Carson-Dellosa

0-7424-2893-1 • Using the Standards–Measurement 3

Name _____ Date _____

# Customary Equivalent

Fill in each blank with the equivalent measurement.

| | | | | | | | |
|---|---|---|---|---|---|---|---|
| **I.** | inches | 12 | 24 | | | 60 | |
| **2.** | feet | 1 | | 3 | | | 6 |

| | | | | | | | |
|---|---|---|---|---|---|---|---|
| **3.** | quarts | 4 | | 12 | | | 24 |
| **4.** | gallons | | 2 | | 4 | | 6 |

| | | | | | | | |
|---|---|---|---|---|---|---|---|
| **5.** | ounces | 16 | | 48 | | | 96 |
| **6.** | pounds | 1 | | 3 | | | 6 |

## DO MORE

Make another chart showing feet and yards. Leave several spaces on your chart blank. See if a classmate can fill in each space.

© Carson-Dellosa                 0-7424-2893-1 • Using the Standards–Measurement 3

Name _____ Date _____

# Metric Equivalent

Fill in each blank with the equivalent measurement.

| **1.** centimeters | 100 | | | 400 | |
| --- | --- | --- | --- | --- | --- |
| **2.** meters | | 2 | | | 5 |

| **3.** milliliters | | | 3,000 | | |
| --- | --- | --- | --- | --- | --- |
| **4.** liters | 1 | 2 | | | 5 |

| **5.** grams | | 2,000 | 3,000 | | |
| --- | --- | --- | --- | --- | --- |
| **6.** kilograms | 1 | | | 4 | |

## DO MORE

Extend each chart. Can you extend the top chart through 1,000 centimeters? Can you extend the bottom chart through 10,000 grams?

© Carson-Dellosa                    0-7424-2893-1 • Using the Standards–Measurement 3

Name _____ Date _____

# Comparing Values

Use <, >, or = to make each sentence true.

**1.** 2 gallons ( ) 8 pints      **2.** 2 pounds ( ) 36 ounces

**3.** 3 feet ( ) 1 yard      **4.** 2 feet ( ) 2 miles

**5.** 2 gallons ( ) 10 quarts      **6.** 18 inches ( ) 6 feet

**7.** 12 inches ( ) 1 foot      **8.** 10 cups ( ) 4 pints

**9.** 3 yards ( ) 1 foot      **10.** 3 quarts ( ) 12 pints

Fill in an amount to make each sentence true.

**11.** 16 ounces = _____

**12.** 1 pint = _____

**13.** 16 cups = _____

**14.** 1 mile = _____

## THINK

Do most people in the United States use metric or customary units?

© Carson-Dellosa      0-7424-2893-1 • Using the Standards–Measurement 3

Name _____ Date _____

# Convert to...

Convert each measurement to inches.

**1.** 4 feet _____

**2.** 12 feet _____

**3.** 6 feet_____

**4.** $8\frac{1}{2}$ feet_____

**5.** $3\frac{1}{2}$ feet_____

Convert each measurement to yards.

**6.** 12 feet _____

**7.** 18 feet _____

**8.** 27 feet _____

**9.** 9 feet _____

**10.** 12 feet _____

Convert each measurement to pounds.

**11.** 16 ounces_____

**12.** 48 ounces_____

**13.** 40 ounces_____

**14.** 64 ounces_____

**15.** 80 ounces_____

## THINK

Think about a time when you might need to convert feet to inches. Think about a time that you might convert ounces to pounds.

© Carson-Dellosa

0-7424-2893-1 • Using the Standards–Measurement 3

Name _____ Date _____

# *From Least to Greatest*

**1.** List the following in order from least to greatest.

pint

quart

gallon

cup _____ _____ _____ _____

**2.** List the following in order from shortest to longest.

foot

yard

inch

mile _____ _____ _____ _____

**3.** List the following in order from longest to shortest.

second

hour

minute

day _____ _____ _____ _____

## DO MORE

Write a story. Include at least three units of measurement in your story.

© Carson-Dellosa   0-7424-2893-1 • Using the Standards–Measurement 3

# Create Your Own Problems I

1. Trace your hand on a piece of graph paper. Trace your foot on a piece of graph paper. Challenge a classmate to find out which has the larger area.

2. Pretend you are 10 feet tall. Write a story about how hard or easy it is to do certain things because of your height. Include what it would be like to visit the grocery store, the doctor's office, or ride on an airplane. Write three questions about your story. Ask a friend to read it and answer the questions.

3. Pretend you are training to run a 10-mile race. Design two practice routes that are each 10 miles. Draw a map showing each route. Try walking or biking each route with an adult or friend.

© Carson-Dellosa

0-7424-2893-1 • Using the Standards–Measurement 3

Name _____  Date _____

# Create Your Own Problems II

1. Draw five things from the grocery store. Have a classmate write the items in order from lightest to heaviest.

2. Design your dream room. It can be a bathroom, study, bedroom, or whatever you like. Include the perimeter of your room and the length of at least five items that you select for your dream room.

3. Check out the sports page of your local newspaper. Find at least three measurements in an article. Create questions to go with these newspaper facts.

© Carson-Dellosa 0-7424-2893-1 • Using the Standards–Measurement 3

Name _____ Date _____

# *Check Your Skills*

**I.** Draw a line measuring $3\frac{1}{2}$ centimeters.

**2.** Draw a line measuring $3\frac{1}{2}$ inches.

Fill in each blank with the most reasonable unit of measurement.

**3.** The distance between my house and my best friend's house is about
2 _____.

     a. inches      b. feet      c. miles      d. grams

**4.** I added $1\frac{1}{2}$ _____ of chocolate chips to the recipe for 3 dozen cookies.

     a. cups      b. gallons      c. yards      d. quarts

**5.** My mom bought a 10 _____ turkey to serve for the holidays.

     a. ounce      b. liter      c. gram      d. pound

**6.** Circle the right angle.

a.       b.       c.

**7.** Find the perimeter of the square below. _____

 $2\frac{1}{2}$ inches

57

© Carson-Dellosa

Name _____ Date _____

# *Check Your Skills (cont.)*

**8.** How many hours are in 150 minutes? _____

Convert each of the following.

**9.** 12 feet = _____ yards

**10.** 18 inches = _____ feet

**11.** 8 cups = _____ quarts

Find the area of each of the following shapes.

**12.**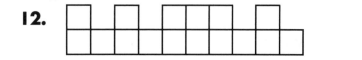

_____

**13.**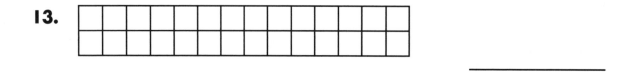

_____

**14.** Draw as many rectangles with an area of 10 square units as you can on a piece of graph paper.

© Carson-Dellosa 0-7424-2893-1 • Using the Standards–Measurement 3

Name _____ Date _____

# Check Your Skills (cont.)

**15.** List one item that might be measured in each of the following units.

a. inches _____

b. yards _____

c. centimeters _____

d. grams _____

e. pounds _____

**16.** Think about the weight of each of the following objects. Then write the objects in order from lightest to heaviest.

wet suit _____

life jacket _____

beach ball _____

lounge chair _____

**17.** Draw a triangle with a perimeter of 12 centimeters on the back of this paper.

**18.** How do you find the perimeter of a shape?

_____

**19.** How do you find the area of a rectangle?

_____

**59**

© Carson-Dellosa

Name _____  Date _____

# Check Your Skills (cont.)

**20.** Tito wants to buy the largest container of orange juice that he can. Which of the following should he purchase?

a. pint          b. quart          c. gallon          d. cup

**21.** List the people that live in your household in order from shortest to tallest.

_____

**22.** How much do the onions weigh? _____

**23.** List three distances that could be measured in miles.

_____

**24.** How much wood will Latoya need to frame a square picture measuring 10 inches on one side?

_____

© Carson-Dellosa
0-7424-2893-1 • Using the Standards–Measurement 3

Name _____ Date _____

# Irregular Perimeter

Find the perimeter of the following irregular shapes.

**1.**

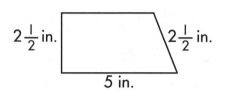

$2\frac{1}{2}$ in.    $2\frac{1}{2}$ in.

5 in.

**2.**

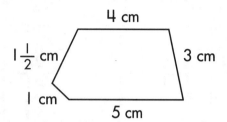

4 cm

$1\frac{1}{2}$ cm    3 cm

1 cm

5 cm

**3.**

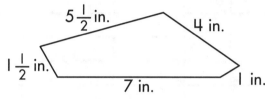

$5\frac{1}{2}$ in.    4 in.

$1\frac{1}{2}$ in.

7 in.    1 in.

**4.**

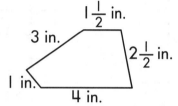

$1\frac{1}{2}$ in.

3 in.    $2\frac{1}{2}$ in.

1 in.

4 in.

**5.**

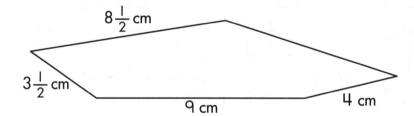

$8\frac{1}{2}$ cm

$3\frac{1}{2}$ cm

9 cm    4 cm

Try to draw two irregular shapes with the following side measurements.

**6.**  $3\frac{1}{2}$ centimeters, 7 centimeters, $8\frac{1}{2}$ centimeters, 2 centimeters, $5\frac{1}{2}$ centimeters

**7.**  $6\frac{1}{2}$ inches, 7 inches, $7\frac{1}{2}$ inches, 5 inches, $3\frac{1}{2}$ inches

## DO MORE

Look around your classroom for an irregular shape. Find the perimeter of the shape.

© Carson-Dellosa    0-7424-2893-1 • Using the Standards–Measurement 3

Name _____ Date _____

# Irregular Shapes

Look at the irregular shapes. Inside each one write its perimeter using units.
Then draw two different irregular shapes, each having a perimeter of 23 units.

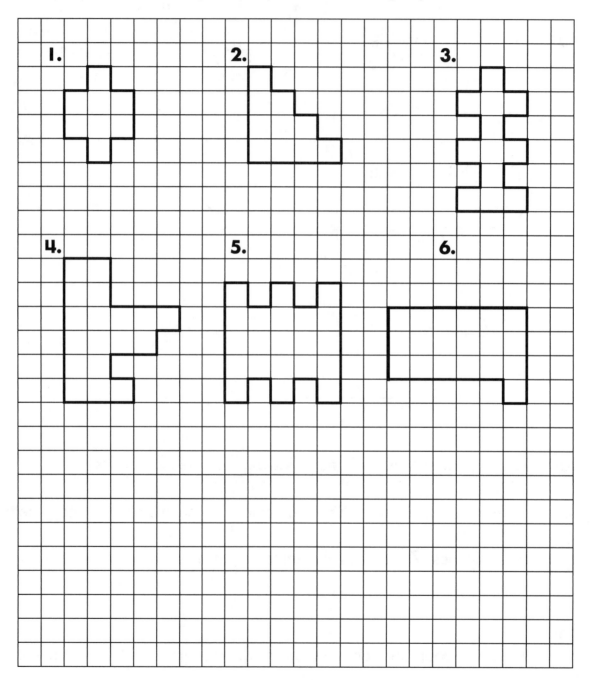

© Carson-Dellosa

0-7424-2893-1 • Using the Standards–Measurement 3

Name _____ Date _____

# *Paper Clip Length*

Use paper clips to measure the length of each of the following lines.

**1.** _____

**2.** _____

**3.** _____

**4.** _____

**5.** _____

## DO MORE

Now measure the length of the paper clip you used to measure each item. Based on this information, what do you think the actual measurement of each line is?

**63**

Name _____ Date _____

# School Measurements

Take a walk around your school. See if you can find items that
you think are about the following lengths. Write down each
guess on the line. Then use a ruler or tape measure to check
your answers.

|  |  | **Prediction** | **Checked** |
|---|---|---|---|
| **1.** | 4 yards | _____ | _____ |
| **2.** | $6\frac{1}{2}$ inches | _____ | _____ |
| **3.** | 4 feet | _____ | _____ |
| **4.** | 3 centimeters | _____ | _____ |
| **5.** | 12 feet | _____ | _____ |
| **6.** | 3 yards | _____ | _____ |

**7.** Write four ways that length measurements are important in sports played on the
playground.

_____

_____

_____

## DO MORE

Create a scavenger hunt for a classmate. Describe in detail three items
around your classroom or school. Include information about their lengths.
Challenge a classmate to find the items that you describe. Set a timer to
make this activity a real challenge.

**64**

Name _____ Date _____

# Neighborhood Map

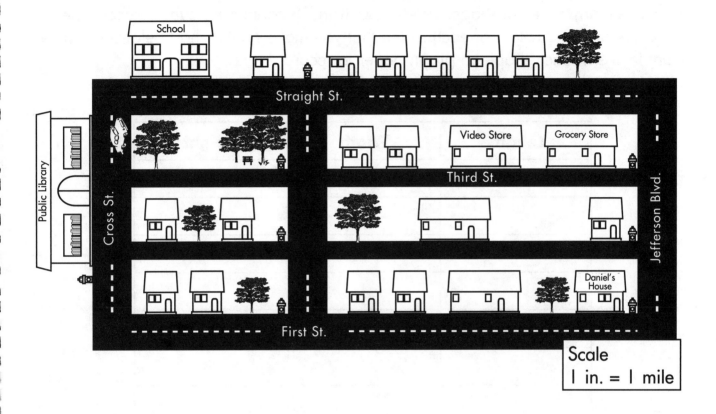

1. About how many miles long is Straight Street?_____

2. Daniel takes the bus to school. About how many miles does he go?_____

3. Daniel walks home from the park with his mom everyday. About how many yards do they walk?_____

4. Daniel's class goes to the library once a month. How many yards do they walk to get there? _____

## THINK

 Why do you think scales on maps are used to show various distances?

© Carson-Dellosa 0-7424-2893-1 • Using the Standards–Measurement 3

Name _____ Date _____

# Cube Shapes

Make as many different shapes as you can with 48 connecting cubes. Record the length, width, and height of each shape that you make on the chart below. You may want to sketch each shape on graph paper to record it.

| Length | Width | Height |
|--------|-------|--------|
|        |       |        |
|        |       |        |
|        |       |        |
|        |       |        |
|        |       |        |
|        |       |        |
|        |       |        |
|        |       |        |
|        |       |        |
|        |       |        |

## DO MORE

Try this activity again. How many rectangles can you make using 16 connecting cubes? Make a chart and record your answers. How many cubes can you make using 64 connecting cubes?

© Carson-Dellosa

0-7424-2893-1 • Using the Standards–Measurement 3

Name _____ Date _____

# Estimating Apples

One and a half apples weigh about 1 pound. Based on this estimation, look at the number of apples on each scale and draw an arrow on each scale to show a good estimate of the weight of the apples shown.

**1.**

**2.**

**3.**

**4.**

**5.**

**6.**

## DO MORE

Pretend apples cost $2.00 a pound. Based on your estimates, how much would each group of apples pictured above cost?

© Carson-Dellosa    0-7424-2893-1 • Using the Standards–Measurement 3

Name _____ Date _____

# *Compare the Weights*

Make a balance scale. Compare the weights of each of the following pairs of objects. Circle the name of the object that weights more.

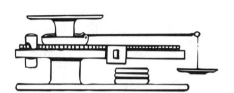

**1.** dictionary                thesaurus

**2.** dictionary                three pens

**3.** six paper clips            six erasers

**4.** stapler                   hole punch

**5.** full lunch box             full lunch bag

**6.** Think of a time when it might be important to know the weights of school tools. Who would want to know the weights and why?

_____

_____

_____

_____

_____

## DO MORE

Use an encyclopedia or the Internet to find the average weight of five of your favorite animals. List these animals in order from least to greatest, based on their weights.

**68**

Name _____ Date _____

# *Grocery Store Weights*

Visit your local grocery store and complete the following five tasks.

**1.**  Weigh five oranges. _____

Based on this information, how much do you think ten oranges would weigh?
_____

**2.**  Weigh 1 pint of strawberries. _____

Based on this information, how much do you think 3 pints of strawberries would weigh?_____

**3.**  About how many apples would make up 1 pound of apples?_____

Based on this information, about how many apples would make up 2 pounds of apples?_____

**4.**  Weigh 2 pounds of tomatoes. _____

Based on this information, about how many tomatoes would make up 3 pounds of tomatoes? _____

**5.**  About how many bananas would make up 2 pounds of bananas? _____

Based on this information, about how many bananas would make up 4 pounds of bananas? _____

## DO MORE

Bananas cost $0.42 per pound. Based on your estimate, figure out about how much you think it would cost to buy 20 bananas.

**69**

Name _____ Date _____

# Surface Area and Volume

Answer the questions below. Draw pictures to help you solve.

**1.** The top face of a cube has an area of 16 square feet. What is the volume of the cube?

**2.** The top face of a rectangular prism is 32 square centimeters, and it is 7 centimeters tall. What is the volume of the rectangular prism?

**3.** The volume of a cube is 8 cubic inches. What is the length of one side?

## DO MORE

Build a shape using 18 connecting cubes. What is the volume of the shape that you built?

**70**

Name _____ Date _____

# *Cube Volume*

Use connecting cubes to create shapes with the following volumes.
Draw each shape you build.

**1.** 23 cubic units

**2.** 33 cubic units

**3.** 9 cubic units

Build five shapes using connecting cubes. Write the volume of each shape that
you build.

**4.** _____        **5.** _____

**6.** _____        **7.** _____

**8.** _____

## DO MORE

Design two different shapes. Make each shape have a volume of
30 cubic units.

© Carson-Dellosa    0-7424-2893-1 • Using the Standards–Measurement 3

Name _____ Date _____

# Rows of Cubes

Use connecting cubes to build the five shapes described on the chart below. Fill in the volume once you have built each shape.

|  | # of rows | # in each row | # of layers | Volume |
|---|---|---|---|---|
| **1.** | 4 | 3 | 2 | |
| **2.** | 5 | 6 | 8 | |
| **3.** | 8 | 4 | 2 | |
| **4.** | 10 | 6 | 4 | |
| **5.** | 4 | 8 | 6 | |
| **6.** | | | | |

## DO MORE

Create a distinctive looking shape on your own. For #6 above, fill in the information from the shape you created. Give the information to a classmate. See if he or she can re-create the same shape based on the information you give in #6. Provide some additional clues, if needed.

**72**

# Creating Volume

Use connecting cubes to complete the following exercises. Create a shape for each volume listed. Draw your shape. Then find the area of the front face.

**1.**  volume = 16 cubic units
area of 1 face = _____

**2.**  volume = 25 cubic units
area of 1 face = _____

**3.**  volume = 14 cubic units
area of 1 face = _____

**4.**  volume = 9 cubic units
area of 1 face = _____

## THINK

Why do you think it is possible to create two different shapes that both have the same volume?

© Carson-Dellosa

0-7424-2893-1 • Using the Standards–Measurement 3

Name _____ Date _____

# *Layers of Volume*

Draw shapes that have the following number of units.
Fill in the volume for each shape.

**1.**   number of rows = 4
number in each row = 2
number of layers = 4

volume _____

**2.**   number of rows = 2
number in each row = 2
number of layers = 5

volume _____

**3.**   number of rows = 5
number in each row = 5
number of layers = 6

volume _____

**THINK**

Why do you need to know the number of layers to find the volume of a shape?

**74**

© Carson-Dellosa

Name _____ Date _____

# Shaded and Un-Shaded

Find the shaded area of each grid.

**1.**

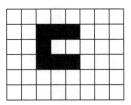

_____

**2.**

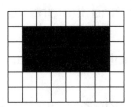

_____

**3.**

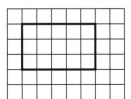

_____

**4.**

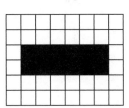

_____

Find the area of each shape.

**5.**

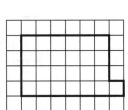

_____

**6.**

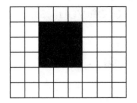

_____

**7.**

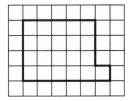

_____

**8.**

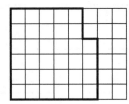

_____

## DO MORE

Use connecting cubes to cover your desk. What is the area of your desk?

© Carson-Dellosa    0-7424-2893-1 • Using the Standards–Measurement 3

Name _____ Date _____

# Cover the Area

Use connecting cubes to find the area of the following five items in your classroom. Do this by covering each of the items listed with connecting cubes. Count the connecting cubes to find the area of each object.

**1.** area of the seat of your chair

**2.** area of the inside of your desk

**3.** area of the sole of your shoe

**4.** area of the reading table

**5.** area of your favorite space to work

**6.** Write about one time you might need to find the area to solve a real-life problem.

_____

_____

_____

_____

_____

_____

## DO MORE

Be a detective. Can you find an object around your classroom with an area of 20 square units? 50 square units?

© Carson-Dellosa     0-7424-2893-1 • Using the Standards–Measurement 3

Name _____ Date _____

# *Draw a Rectangle*

On another piece of paper, draw a picture of each of the rectangles described below. Then find the area of each rectangle.

**1.**   length = 9 centimeters       width = 4 centimeters

area = _____

**2.**   length = 2 inches       width = 5 inches

area = _____

**3.**   length = 10 inches       width = 3 inches

area = _____

**4.**   length = 3 centimeters       width = 7 centimeters

area = _____

**5.**   length = 1 centimeter       width = 1 centimeter

area = _____

**6.**   length = 3 inches       width = 5 inches

area = _____

## THINK

Why do you have to know the length and width of a rectangle to find its area?

© Carson-Dellosa

0-7424-2893-1 • Using the Standards–Measurement 3

Name _____ Date _____

# Graph Shapes

Draw a shape with each area listed on each section of graph paper below.

**1.**  7 square units

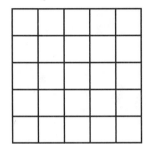

**2.**  12 square units

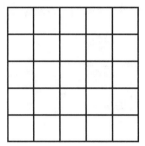

**3.**  21 square units

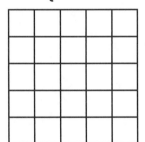

**4.**  4 square units

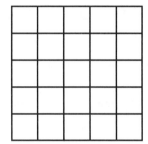

**5.**  15 square units

**6.**  10 square units

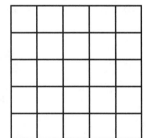

## DO MORE

On a sheet of graph paper create a picture. Everything in your picture should add up to 40 square units of area.

© Carson-Dellosa

# Fill in the Area

Look at the information on the chart. Fill in the area for each of the rectangles described. To help you, draw each rectangle described on the chart.

| | # of rows | # of columns | Area |
|---|---|---|---|
| **1.** | 2 | 5 | |
| **2.** | 1 | 2 | |
| **3.** | 4 | 2 | |
| **4.** | 7 | 5 | |
| **5.** | 3 | 3 | |
| **6.** | 8 | 2 | |
| **7.** | 4 | 10 | |
| **8.** | 9 | 8 | |

**THINK**

What formula did you use to find the area of each rectangle?

© Carson-Dellosa

0-7424-2893-1 • Using the Standards–Measurement 3

Name _____ Date _____

# The Area of Shapes

On the graph paper, draw shapes with the following areas.

**1.** 10 square units

**2.** 30 square units

**3.** 24 square units

**4.** 12 square units

**5.** 18 square units

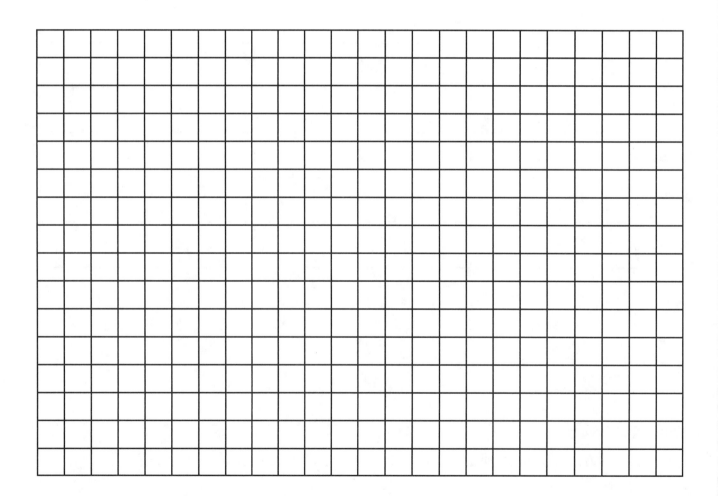

© Carson-Dellosa   0-7424-2893-1 • Using the Standards–Measurement 3

Name _____ Date _____

# Cut Out Shapes

Use scissors to cut out of graph paper each of the shapes described below. Write the area on the back of each shape.

**1.** Cut out a rectangle with 3 rows and 3 columns.

**2.** Cut out a rectangle with 5 rows and 2 columns.

**3.** Cut out a rectangle with 6 rows and 8 columns.

**4.** Cut out a rectangle with 10 rows and 10 columns.

**5.** Cut out a rectangle with 4 rows and 6 columns.

**6.** Cut out a rectangle with 9 rows and 8 columns.

**7.** a. Draw a rectangle with an area of 20 square units.

b. Draw a square with an area of 9 square units.

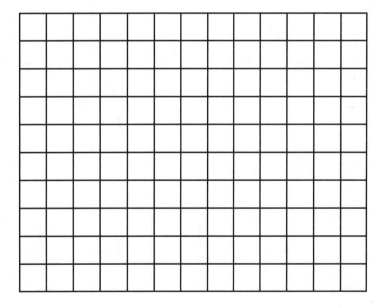

## DO MORE

Tape together three of your shapes. What is the area now?

© Carson-Dellosa

Name _____ Date _____

# *José's Room*

José is about to move into a new house. Before the move his mom gives him a floor plan of his new room and some cut-outs of his furniture. She asks him to glue each piece of furniture on the floor plan so that the movers will place José's furniture in a way that he will like. Cut out each piece of furniture and glue it on the floor plan. Then answer the questions on the following page.

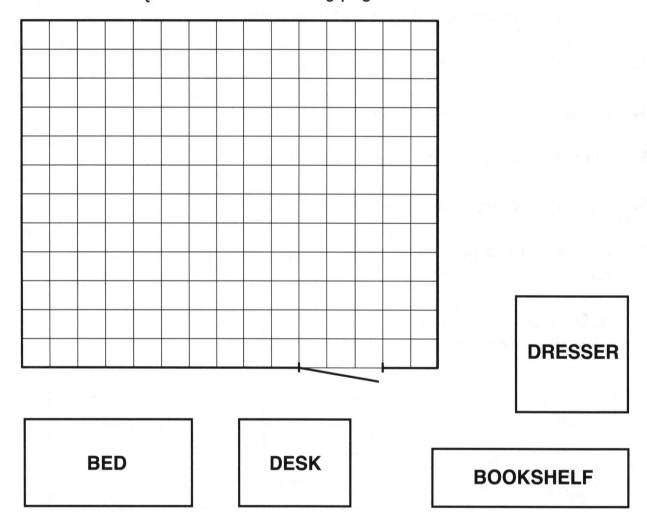

DRESSER

BED

DESK

BOOKSHELF

## DO MORE

Measure your room. Draw your room on a sheet of graph paper. Draw the furniture in your room on your room outline.

© Carson-Dellosa

0-7424-2893-1 • Using the Standards–Measurement 3

Name _____ Date _____

# José's Room (cont.)

Answer the following questions after you complete page 82.

**1.** What is the area of José's room? _____

**2.** How much space will José's bed take up? _____

**3.** Where did you place José's bookshelf? Why? _____

_____

**4.** What is the area of José's dresser? _____

**5.** José's bookshelf is 2 units wide by 7 units long. His books take up an area of 10 square units. How much space does he have left on the shelf? _____

**6.** How much space does José's furniture take up in all? _____

**7.** What is the area of your room? Is your room smaller or larger than José's room? How do you know? _____

_____

_____

**THINK**

How can having a floor plan of a room be helpful?

© Carson-Dellosa

0-7424-2893-1 • Using the Standards–Measurement 3

Name _____ Date _____

# Shape Riddles

Read the description of each shape. Then draw the correct shape in each box. Write the area on the line.

**1.**  I am a rectangle. I have 6 rows and 8 columns.

   area = _____

**2.**  I am a square. I have 8 colums and 8 rows.

   area = _____

**3.**  I am a rectangle. I have 4 rows and 3 columns.

   area = _____

## DO MORE

Describe a shape. Challenge a classmate to draw it. What is the area of the shape you described? What is the perimeter?

© Carson-Dellosa

Name _____ Date _____

# *Tile Shapes*

Use six colored tiles to create five different shapes. Draw each shape and write the area beside it.

**1.**                                                     area = _____

**2.**                                                     area = _____

**3.**                                                     area = _____

**4.**                                                     area = _____

**5.**                                                     area = _____

**6.**   What do you notice about the area of each? _____

_____

## DO MORE

Are any of the floors in your home covered in tile? If yes, count the number of tiles in the room using "tiles" as your non-standard unit of measurement. What is the area of the floor?

© Carson-Dellosa

Name _____ Date _____

# The Right Angle

This └ is a right angle. For each angle below, write >, <, or = to compare it to a right angle. The greater than symbol means it is more than 90°. The less than symbol means it is less than 90°. The equals symbol means it is equal to 90°.

**1.**

**2.**

**3.**

**4.**

**5.**

**6.**

**7.**

**8.**

**THINK**

How do you know if an angle equals 90°?

© Carson-Dellosa

0-7424-2893-1 • Using the Standards–Measurement 3

# Greater and Less Than 90°

**1.** Circle all the angles that are greater than 90°.

**2.** Put a line through all the angles that are less than 90°.

**3.** Box all the angles that are 90°.

a.
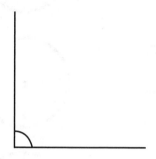

b.

c.
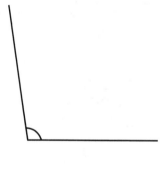

d.
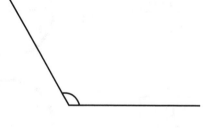

e.
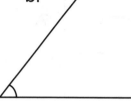

f.
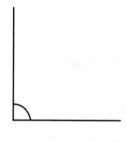

g.

h.

i.

## DO MORE

Use a protractor to draw a 90° angle. Draw an angle that is less than 90°. Draw an angle that is more than 90°.

© Carson-Dellosa 0-7424-2893-1 • Using the Standards–Measurement 3

Name _____  Date _____

# Matching Clocks

Draw lines to connect matching clocks.

**1.** 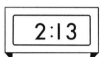 2:13  a.

b.

**2.** 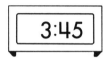 3:45  **7.** 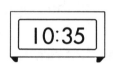 11:45

c.

**3.**  4:30  h.

d.

**4.**  5:00  **8.**  12:15  i.

e.

**6.**  10:35  f.

g.

**9.**  12:45  j.

**5.**  9:20

**10.**  5:30

## DO MORE

List the times above in order from earliest to latest, starting at 12:00.

© Carson-Dellosa

0-7424-2893-1 • Using the Standards–Measurement 3

Name _____ Date _____

# Time Zones

There are four different time zones across the continental United States: Eastern, Central, Mountain, and Pacific. Look at the map below. Then answer the questions.

**Time Zones in the 48 Contiguous States**

1. Janissa is flying from Cincinnati to Madison. Will she turn her watch forward or backward? _____

2. Kamal takes the train from San Francisco to Denver and then to Little Rock. How many times does he need to change his watch? _____ Will he turn it forward or backward? _____

3. Renee lives in Atlanta. She wants to call her cousin in Salem, but she can't call until 9:00 A.M. Salem time. It is 10:00 A.M. right now in Atlanta. How many hours will she have to wait to call? _____

**THINK**

What time zone do you live in?

© Carson-Dellosa   0-7424-2893-1 • Using the Standards–Measurement 3

Name _____ Date _____

# Show the Temperature

Fill in each thermometer with the temperature listed. Read each thermometer. On another piece of paper, write one sentence describing the temperature and one sentence describing the clothes you might choose to wear based on the temperature.

**1.** 20°F

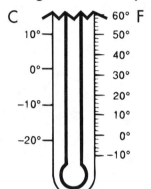

**2.** 40°C

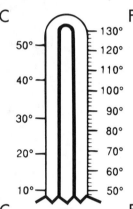

**3.** 32°F

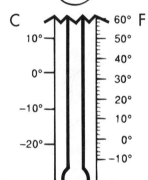

**4.** 101°F

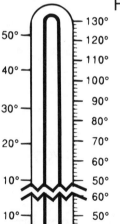

**5.** 0°C

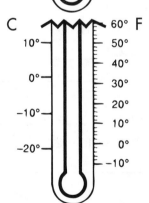

**6.** 50°F

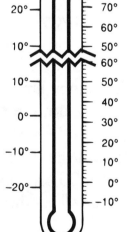

## DO MORE

Use your local newspaper to find and record the daily temperature in your city for one week. Make a line graph showing this information.

© Carson-Dellosa

0-7424-2893-1 • Using the Standards—Measurement 3

Name _____ Date _____

# *Temperature Tool*

**1.** Why are thermometers important tools?

_____

_____

**2.** How does knowing the temperature help people?

_____

_____

**3.** Write a list of some of your favorite things to do when it is between 75 and 85 degrees Fahrenheit.

_____

_____

**4.** Write a list of some of your favorite things to do when it is between 30 and 40 degrees Fahrenheit.

_____

_____

## THINK

Why do you think many people like to watch the news and learn about the weather before they go to sleep at night? Do you like to watch and learn about the weather? Why or why not?

**91**

Name _____ Date _____

# Draw the Perimeter

Follow the directions below. You may need to draw on another piece of paper.

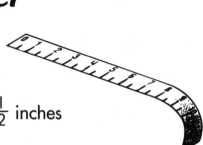

1. Draw an irregular shape that has a perimeter of $19\frac{1}{2}$ inches

2. Draw an irregular shape that has a perimeter of 27 centimeters.

3. Draw an irregular shape that has an area of 21 square units.

4. Draw an irregular shape that has an area of 38 square units.

5. Draw an irregular shape that has a volume of 41 cubic units.

6. Draw an irregular shape that has a volume of 11 cubic units.

**THINK**

You are designing a new garden in front of your house. You are trying to decide how many flowers to buy for your garden. Do you think knowing the perimeter, area, or volume will help you the most? Why?

© Carson-Dellosa   0-7424-2893-1 • Using the Standards–Measurement 3

Name _____ Date _____

# *Choose a Tool*

Match each measurement to the picture of the tool you need to use.

**1.** length of an envelope

**2.** weight of an apple versus an orange

**3.** time you need to arrive at dance class

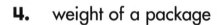

**4.** weight of a package

**5.** amount of fabric needed to make a skirt

**6.** amount of wood needed to build
an 8-foot tall bookcase

**THINK**

How are scales used in the grocery store or in the post office?

© Carson-Dellosa   0-7424-2893-1 • Using the Standards–Measurement 3

Name _____  Date _____

# What's an Estimate?

**1.**   People estimate distances, lengths, and weights when they are not sure of an exact answer. There are many times when an estimate is needed but an exact answer is not necessary. List three examples when you might be able to use an estimate rather than an exact answer in measurement.

a.   _____

b.   _____

c.   _____

**2.**   What is the difference between an estimate and an exact answer?

_____

_____

**3.**   Can you think of a time when an exact answer would be necessary and an estimate would not provide enough information? List three examples when you could not use an estimate.

a.   _____

b.   _____

c.   _____

## DO MORE

Estimate the amount of time it takes you to get ready for school. Then have an adult help you time yourself one morning. Was your estimate close?

© Carson-Dellosa   0-7424-2893-1 • Using the Standards–Measurement 3

Name _____ Date _____

# Perimeter and Area

Find the perimeter and area for each shape.

**1.**

perimeter _____

area _____

**2.**

perimeter _____

area _____

**3.**

perimeter _____

area _____

**4.**

perimeter _____

area _____

**5.**

perimeter _____

area _____

**6.**

perimeter _____

area _____

## THINK

If the perimeter of a rectangle stays constant at 25 feet, what happens to the area as the shape becomes less long and thin and more like a square?

© Carson-Dellosa

Name _____ Date _____

# Shape Designs

Draw six shapes on the graph paper. Write the area and perimeter on each of your shapes. One example is provided below. Add color to your design, if you like.

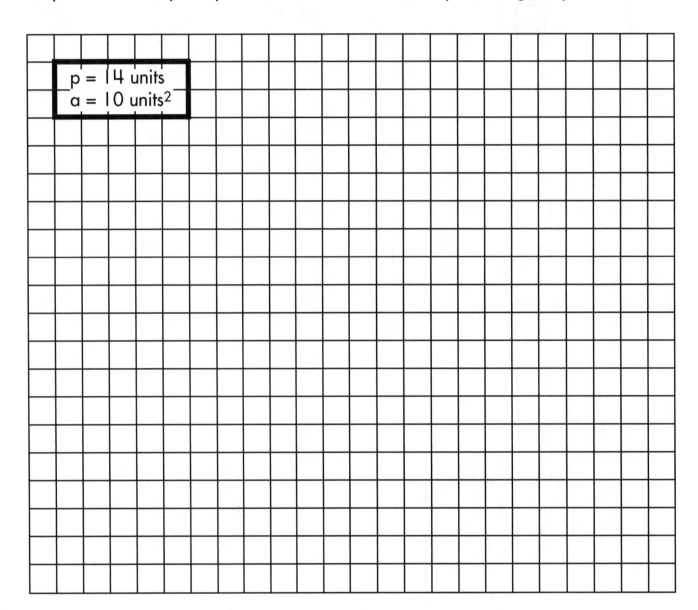

p = 14 units
a = 10 units$^2$

## DO MORE

On another piece of paper, create another design. Challenge a classmate to add the correct perimeter and area to each shape on your design. Check his or her work.

© Carson-Dellosa

0-7424-2893-1 • Using the Standards–Measurement 3

Name _____ Date _____

# *Block Letters*

On each section of graph paper write the word given in block letters. Write the area of each word on the line provided.

**1.** hi

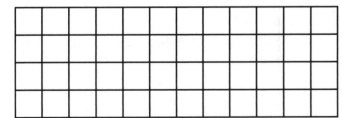

Area _____

**2.** math

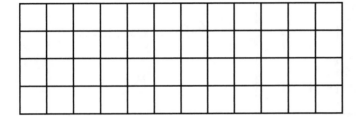

Area _____

**3.** area

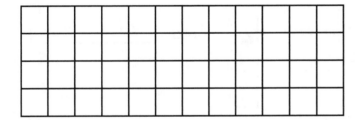

Area _____

## DO MORE

Write a word of your choice on a sheet of graph paper. What is the area of your word?

© Carson-Dellosa

0-7424-2893-1 • Using the Standards–Measurement 3

Name _____ Date _____

# *Graphing Words*

On each section of graph paper write the word given in block letters. Write the area of each word on the line provided.

**1.**   fun

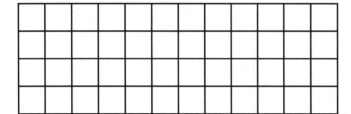

Area _____

**2.**   learn

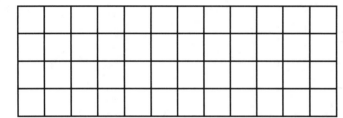

Area _____

**3.**   dance

Area _____

## THINK

Which word had the greatest area? List the words in order from least amount of area to greatest amount of area.

© Carson-Dellosa   0-7424-2893-1 • Using the Standards–Measurement 3

Name _____ Date _____

# *Outdoor Area*

Time for an outdoor adventure! Take a bag of connecting cubes outside with a partner. Select five surfaces outside. Work on each surface one at a time. First, cover your surface with connecting cubes. Then count the number of connecting cubes it took to cover each surface. What is the area of each surface? Describe each surface and write the area of each surface below.

**1.** _____

_____

**2.** _____

_____

**3.** _____

_____

**4.** _____

_____

**5.** _____

## THINK

Does knowing the area of a space help you have a better understanding of its size? Why or why not?

© Carson-Dellosa

Name _____ Date _____

# *What Are You Measuring?*

Read each question. Write several sentences explaining your answer.

**1.** To measure a piece of paper to create a drawing, will you be measuring volume, area, or distance? Why?

_____

_____

_____

**2.** To measure a quantity of sugar for a recipe, will you be measuring volume, area, or distance? Why?

_____

_____

_____

**3.** To measure a route between your house and your school, will you be measuring volume, area, or distance? Why?

_____

_____

_____

## DO MORE

Write your own question like the ones above. Challenge a friend to solve it.

© Carson-Dellosa    0-7424-2893-1 • Using the Standards–Measurement 3

Name _____ Date _____

# *Measuring Words*

Use a dictionary to look up the following words

**1.** surface area _____

_____

_____

**2.** volume _____

_____

_____

**3.** What is the difference between surface and volume?

_____

_____

**4.** Do you think it is easier to find the surface area or the volume of a shape?

Why?

_____

_____

## DO MORE

Write about what you learned about surface area and volume from completing the activities in this section.

© Carson-Dellosa    0-7424-2893-1 • Using the Standards–Measurement 3

Name _____  Date _____

# *Create Your Own Problems I*

**1.** Choose a place you have always wanted to visit. Use the Internet to find the average temperature during this time of year. Use this information to write a story about the clothes that you will pack so you are comfortable on your trip.

**2.** Use connecting cubes to find the area of two different surfaces where you might do your homework. What is the difference in area between the two surfaces? On which surface do you prefer to do your homework? Why?

**3.** Poll your classmates. Do most of them have digital or analog alarm clocks? Record this information and make a chart to show your findings. Do you have a digital or an analog clock next to your bed? Why?

**4.** Find ten things around your classroom that are smaller than 1 foot. Use a ruler to measure each one.

© Carson-Dellosa  0-7424-2893-1 • Using the Standards–Measurement 3

Name _____ Date _____

# *Create Your Own Problems II*

**1.** You are making sandwiches and cookies for your class. How many pounds of lunchmeat will you need to buy? How many loaves of bread? How many dozen cookies will you need to bake? Write your grocery list below.

**2.** Write a story about "Elsie the Estimator." Make sure you include at least five things that Elsie estimates.

**3.** Visit your local post office. Find out about some of the rates that they charge for mailing packages of different sizes and weights.

**4.** Pretend you are redecorating your kitchen. What sorts of measurements do you think you will need to take before you redecorate? Why?

© Carson-Dellosa 0-7424-2893-1 • Using the Standards–Measurement 3

Name _____  Date _____

# Create Your Own Problems III

**1.** Write three word problems for a classmate to solve. Two word problems should have to do with length and one should have to do with weight.

**2.** Pretend you are designing the perfect bedroom. What would the dimensions of your room be? What furniture and types of things would you have in your room? Draw a picture of your perfect bedroom on a sheet of graph paper.

**3.** Pretend you are a sportswriter. Write an article for the sports page. Include at least three units of measurement in your article.

**4.** Build a unique shape using connecting cubes. Record the volume of your shape. Write a brief description of your shape. See if a partner can rebuild your shape based on the information that you provide.

© Carson-Dellosa

0-7424-2893-1 • Using the Standards–Measurement 3

Name _____ Date _____

# Check Your Skills

**1.** Ellie eats a bowl of cereal for breakfast. Which of the following serving sizes is the most reasonable?

    a. 6 ounces       b. 18 ounces       c. 54 ounces

**2.** About how many hours do most people sleep a day?

    a. 2–4 hours      b. 7–9 hours      c. 14–16 hours

**3.** Which temperature is shown on the thermometer?
a. 49 degrees Fahrenheit
b. 89 degrees Fahrenheit
c. 98 degrees Fahrenheit

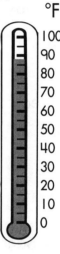

**4.** About how many paper clips long is the straw?

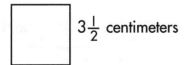

    a. $4\frac{1}{2}$      b. 5      c. $6\frac{1}{2}$

**5.** Find the perimeter of the shape shown.

 $3\frac{1}{2}$ centimeters

    a. 14 cm      b. $8\frac{1}{2}$ cm      c. 11 cm

© Carson-Dellosa      0-7424-2893-1 • Using the Standards–Measurement 3

Name _____ Date _____

# Check Your Skills (cont.)

**6.** Which of the following shapes has a volume of 9 cubic units?

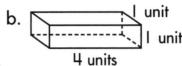

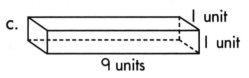

a.

2 units

3 units

b.

1 unit

1 unit

4 units

c.

1 unit

1 unit

9 units

**7.** A ruler would most likely be used to measure the distance between _____ .

a. two cities      b. two classrooms      c. two fingers

**8.** What is the area of the rectangle?

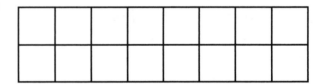

a. 16 square units      b. 12 square units      c. 18 square units

**9.** Assuming one banana weighs about $\frac{1}{2}$ a pound, which scale shows the amount that 6 bananas might weigh?

a. 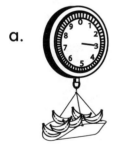      b.       c.

**10.** Which shape has a volume of 16 cubic units?

a.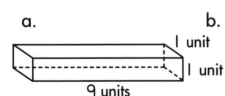

1 unit

1 unit

9 units

b.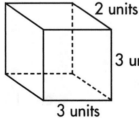

2 units

3 units

3 units

c.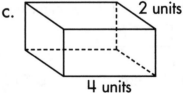

2 units

4 units

© Carson-Dellosa

0-7424-2893-1 • Using the Standards–Measurement 3

Name _____ Date _____

# *Check Your Skills (cont.)*

**11.** A balance scale might best be used to _____.
a. weigh one object
b. compare the weights of two objects
c. compare the lengths of two objects

**12.** Look at the ruler. What is the length of the box?

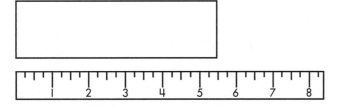

a. 6        b. $5\frac{1}{2}$        c. 5

**13.** Which rectangle has a perimeter of 18 feet?

a. [ ] 3 feet   6 feet        b. [ ] 4 feet   8 feet        c. [ ] 6 feet

**14.** Which formula should Penelope use to find the area of her bedroom?

a. base x height        b. length x width        c. length + height

**15.** The clock shows the time that Marcus leaves to catch the bus. What time does Marcus leave to catch the bus?
a. 2:15
b. 2:45
c. 3:45

© Carson-Dellosa        0-7424-2893-1 • Using the Standards–Measurement 3

# Check Your Skills (cont.)

**16.** Which formula could you use to find the perimeter of the square?

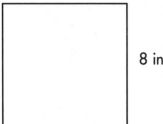

8 inches

a. 8 – 4          b. 8 + 4          c. 8 x 4

**17.** The volume of the shape is _____ cubic units.

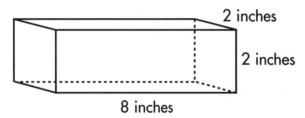

2 inches

2 inches

8 inches

a. 32          b. 34          c. 18

**18.** How many minutes are in 3 hours?

a. 175          b. 180          c. 300

**19.** How many feet are in 60 inches?

a. 4          b. 5          c. 6

**20.** How many cups are in 6 pints?

a. 8          b. 12          c. 18

© Carson-Dellosa

0-7424-2893-1 • Using the Standards–Measurement 3

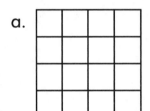

# Post Test

**1.** About how many centimeters are in 4 inches?

   a. 6           b. 10           c. 12

**2.** Circle the square that has the least number of square units.

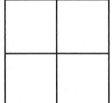      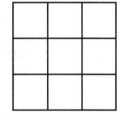

**3.** Which of the following would not be used to measure weight?

   a. grams           b. pounds           c. millimeters

**4.** What is the area of the shape?
   a. 18 square units
   b. 25 square units
   c. 32 square units

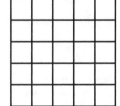

**5.** What is the perimeter of the shape?
   a. 24 inches
   b. 27 inches
   c. 28 inches

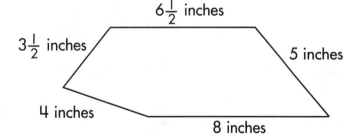

**6.** Circle the right angle.

   a.           b.           c.

© Carson-Dellosa          0-7424-2893-1 • Using the Standards–Measurement 3

# Post Test (cont.)

**7.** Which scale shows $4\frac{1}{2}$ pounds?

a. 　　　b. 　　　c.

**8.** Jamal leaves for his piano lesson at 4:15. Which clock shows the time that Jamal leaves for his lesson?

a. 　　　b. 　　　c.

**9.** Which shape has a volume of 32 cubic units?

a. 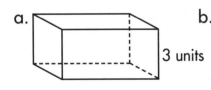　3 units

b. 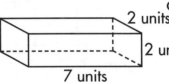　7 units　2 units

c. 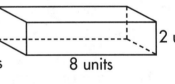　2 units　2 units　8 units

**10.** How many quarts are in 4 gallons? _____

**11.** Josie spends 6 hours at school. How many minutes does Josie spend at school?

a. 260　　　b. 360　　　c. 380

**12.** How do you find the perimeter of a shape?
a. length x width
b. add all sides
c. add all sides and divide by four

**110**

# Answer Key

1. c
2. b
3. b
4. d
5. b
6. d
7. c
8. c
9. b
10. c
11. c
12. b

Answers will vary.

1. a or b
2. d
3. b
4. d
5. b or c
6. a or d
7. inch or foot
8. foot or yard

Answers will vary.

Answers will vary. Answers may include the size of each tool and whether the size ever varies.

Answers will vary.

1. inches
2. miles
3. feet
4. inches
5. yards
6. miles
7. feet
8. yards
9. feet
10. inches

Answers will vary.

1. 3 inches
2. 4 inches
3. 5 inches
4. $1\frac{1}{2}$ inches
5. 2 inches
6. $2\frac{1}{2}$ inches
7. 6 inches
8. $5\frac{1}{2}$ inches

1. $3\frac{1}{2}$ cm line
2. 4 cm line
3. 6 cm line
4. $8\frac{1}{2}$ cm line
5. 7 cm line
6. $9\frac{1}{2}$ cm line

Answers will vary.

Answers will vary.

© Carson-Dellosa

# Answer Key

Answers will vary.

The $2\frac{1}{2}$ -in. string is about 3 mm longer than the 6-cm string.

Answers will vary.

Answers will vary.

1. $7\frac{1}{2}$ cm
2. 14 in.
3. 9 cm
4. $10\frac{1}{2}$ in.
5. 14 in.
6. 34 in.
7. 30 cm
8. 15 ft.

Shapes will vary.

1. pentagon with $3\frac{1}{2}$ cm sides
2. octagon with $8\frac{1}{2}$ cm sides
3. equilateral triangle with $1\frac{1}{2}$ in. sides
4. hexagon with $5\frac{1}{2}$ cm sides
5. shape with a perimeter of 10 cm

1. 1,500 ft.
2. $80.00
3. 700 ft.
4. 11
5. 144 in.

Answers will vary.

1. d
2. a
3. a
4. b
5. d
6. b

1. toy penguin
2. dog
3. man
4. bag of chips
5. armchair

1. ounces
2. pounds
3. pounds
4. ounce
5. ounces

6–8. Drawings will vary.

Answers are approximate.
1. grams
2. grams
3. kilograms
4. grams
5. grams

6.–9. Answers will vary.

1. 2 lb.
2. $3\frac{1}{2}$ lb.
3. 4 lb.

© Carson-Dellosa 0-7424-2893-1 • Using the Standards–Measurement 3

# Answer Key

**4.** $5\frac{1}{4}$ lb.

**5.** $1\frac{1}{2}$ lb.

**6.** $2\frac{1}{2}$ lb.

5, 1, 6, 2, 3, 4

## Prism Volume ..................................33

**1.** 3 cubic units

**2.** 64 cubic units

**3.** 48 cubic units

**4.** 320 cubic units

**5.** 8 cubic units

**6.** 8 cubic units

**7.** 40 cubic units

**8.** 90 cubic units

**9.** 16 cubic units

**10.** 36 cubic units

## Find the Volume ..............................34

**1.** 120 cubic units

**2.** 27 cubic units

**3.** 100 cubic units

**4.** 80 cubic units

**5.** 1 cubic unit

**6.** 2 x 2 x 2 cube

**7.** 1 x 2 x 4 prism

## Customary Capacity ..........................35

**1.** cups

**2.** gallons

**3.** gallon

**4.** cup

**5.** cup

**6.** pint

**7.** quart

**8.** gallon

## Metric Capacity .............................36

**1.** milliliters

**2.** milliliters

**3.** liters

**4.** liters

**5.** grams

**6.** kilograms

**7.** gram

**8.** kilograms

## Comparing Capacity .........................37

**1.** 6

**2.** 8

**3.** 8

**4.** 6

**5.** 16

**6.** 24

**7.** 6

**8.** 10

**9.** 2

**10.** 24

## Find the Area ..............................38

**1.** 10 square units

**2.** 18 square units

**3.** 25 square units

**4.** 8 square units

**5.** 10 square units

**6.** 20 square units

**7.** 6 square units

**8.** 12 square units

## Shape Area ...............................39

Answers will vary.

© Carson-Dellosa

# Answer Key

## Bedroom Map .......................................... 40
1. Desk should be 10 square units and should be placed by a window.
2. Dresser should be 12 square units.

## Reflecting Area ................................... 41
1. area 1 = 5 square units
   area 2 = 10 square units
2. area 1 = 5 square units
   area 2 = 10 square units
3. area 1 = 2 square units
   area 2 = 4 square units
4. area 1 = 4 square units
   area 2 = 8 square units

## Square Units ........................................ 42
1. 20 square inches
2. 8 square feet
3. 4 square inches
4. 40 square centimeters
5. 9 square inches
6. 10 square centimeters
7. 1 square centimeter
8. 35 square centimeters
9. 27 square feet
10. 36 square inches

## Matching Area ..................................... 43
1. 10 square units
2. 12 square units
3. 18 square units
4. 4 square units
5. 20 square units
6. 22 square units
7. 6 square units

## Create an Area .................................... 44
Answers will vary.

## Workout Time ...................................... 45
16 hours, 50 minutes

## How Long Does It Take? ..................... 46
Answers will vary.

## Angle Degrees ..................................... 47
1. right angle
2. greater than right angle
3. less than right angle
4. greater than right angle
5. less than right angle

## Convert the Units ................................ 48
1. 3
2. 144
3. 1
4. 4
5. 72
6. 2
7. 8
8. 1
9. 64
10. 2
11. 6

## Equivalent Units ................................... 49
1. f
2. g
3. d
4. a
5. h
6. b
7. e
8. c
9.–11. Answers will vary.

© Carson-Dellosa

0-7424-2893-1 • Using the Standards–Measurement 3

# Answer Key

**Customary Equivalent ..................... 50**

  **1.** 36, 48, 72

  2. 2, 4, 5

  **3.** 8, 16, 20

  **4.** 1, 3, 5

  **5.** 32, 64, 80

  **6.** 2, 4, 5

**Metric Equivalent ........................ 51**

  **1.** 200, 300, 500

  **2.** 1, 3, 4

  **3.** 1,000, 2,000, 4,000, 5,000

  **4.** 3, 4

  **5.** 1,000, 4,000, 5,000

  **6.** 2, 3, 5

**Comparing Values ....................... 52**

  **1.** >

  **2.** <

  **3.** =

  **4.** <

  **5.** <

  **6.** <

  **7.** =

  **8.** >

  **9.** >

**10.** <

Answers may vary.

**11.** 1 pound

**12.** 2 cups

**13.** 1 gallon

**14.** 5,280 feet

**Convert to............................... 53**

  **1.** 48 in.

  **2.** 144 in.

  3. 72 in.

  **4.** 102 in.

  **5.** 42 in.

  **6.** 4 yd.

  **7.** 6 yd.

  **8.** 9 yd.

  **9.** 3 yd.

**10.** 4 yd.

**11.** 1 lb.

**12.** 3 lb.

**13.** $2\frac{1}{2}$ lb.

**14.** 4 lb.

**15.** 5 lb.

**From Least to Greatest ..................... 54**

  **1.** cup, pint, quart, gallon

  **2.** inch, foot, yard, mile

  **3.** day, hour, minute, second

**Create Your Own Problems ............... 55–56**

Answers will vary.

**Check Your Skills ...................... 57–60**

  **1.** $3\frac{1}{2}$ cm line

  **2.** $3\frac{1}{2}$ in. line

  **3.** c or b

  **4.** a

  **5.** d

  **6.** a

  **7.** 10 in.

  **8.** $2\frac{1}{2}$ hours

  **9.** 4

**10.** $1\frac{1}{2}$ ft.

**11.** 2 qt.

© Carson-Dellosa

# Answer Key

**12.** 16 square units

**13.** 28 square units

**14.** Answers will vary.

**15.** Answers will vary.

**16.** beach ball, life jacket, wet suit, lounge chair

**17.** triangle with perimeter of 12 cm

**18.** add the sides

**19.** length x width

**20.** c

**21.** Answers will vary.

**22.** $4\frac{1}{2}$ lb.

**23.** Answers will vary.

**24.** 40 in.

**1.** 14 in.

**2.** $14\frac{1}{2}$ cm

**3.** 19 in.

**4.** 12 in.

**5.** 33 cm

**6.** Shapes will vary.

**7.** Shapes will vary.

**1.** 14 units

**2.** 16 units

**3.** 26 units

**4.** 24 units

**5.** 28 units

**6.** 20 units

Answers are approximate.

**1.** 2 standard paper clip lengths

**2.** $3\frac{1}{2}$ standard paper clip lengths

**3.** $2\frac{1}{2}$ standard paper clip lengths

**4.** $2\frac{1}{4}$ standard paper clip lengths

**5.** $1\frac{1}{4}$ standard paper clip lengths

Answers will vary.

Answers are approximate.

**1.** $6\frac{1}{4}$ miles

**2.** $7\frac{1}{2}$ miles

**3.** 10,120 yards

**4.** 3,080 yards

Answers will vary.

**1.** $2\frac{1}{2}$ lb.

**2.** 2 lb.

**3.** $5\frac{1}{3}$ lb.

**4.** 4 lb.

**5.** 6 lb.

**6.** $3\frac{1}{3}$ lb.

Answers will vary.

Answers will vary.

**1.** 64 cubic feet

**2.** 224 cubic centimeters

**3.** 2 inches

Answers will vary.

Answers will vary.

Answers will vary.

© Carson-Dellosa

0-7424-2893-1 • Using the Standards–Measurement 3

# Answer Key

**Layers of Volume**.............................**74**
1. 32 cubic units
2. 20 cubic units
3. 150 cubic units

**Shaded and Un-Shaded** ............**75**
1. 7 square units
2. 18 square units
3. 12 square units
4. 9 square units
5. 15 square units
6. 21 square units
7. 25 square units
8. 34 square units

**Cover the Area** ............................**76**
Answers will vary.

**Draw a Rectangle** .......................**77**
1. 36 square centimeters
2. 10 square inches
3. 30 square inches
4. 21 square centimeters
5. 1 square centimeter
6. 15 square inches

**Graph Shapes**...............................**78**
Answers will vary.

**Fill in the Area** ............................**79**
Answers will vary.

**The Area of Shapes**......................**80**
Answers will vary.

**Cut Out Shapes** ...........................**81**
Answers will vary.

**José's Room** ............................**82–83**
1. 180 sq. units
2. 18 sq. units
3. Answers will vary.

4. 16 sq. units
5. 4 sq. units
6. 60 sq. units
7. Answers will vary.

**Shape Riddles** ..............................**84**
1. 48 square units
2. 64 square units
3. 12 square units

**Tile Shapes** ..................................**85**
Answers will vary.

**The Right Angle** ...........................**86**
1. >
2. >
3. =
4. <
5. =
6. <
7. <
8. >

**Greater and Less Than 90°**........**87**
1. d, f, i
2. b, c, g
3. a, e, h

**Matching Clocks** ..........................**88**
1. b
2. d
3. c
4. e
5. a
6. j
7. f
8. i
9. h
10. g

**117**

# Answer Key

**Time Zones** ...................................... **89**
1. backward
2. two times; forward
3. 2 hours

**Show the Temperature** .................... **90**
1. 20°F
2. 40°C
3. 32°F
4. 101°F
5. 0°C
6. 50°F

**Temperature Tool** ........................... **91**
Answers will vary.

**Draw the Perimeter** ....................... **92**
Answers will vary.

**Choose a Tool** ................................ **93**
1. ruler
2. balance scale
3. clock
4. scale
5. yardstick
6. tape measure

**What's an Estimate?** ...................... **94**
1. Answers will vary.
2. An estimate is a logical guess. An actual answer is a calculated answer.
3. Answers will vary.

**Perimeter and Area** ........................ **95**
1. p = 12 units, a = 8 square units
2. p = 12 units, a = 9 square units
3. p = 26 units, a = 30 square units
4. p = 20 units, a = 24 square units
5. p = 20 units, a = 21 square units
6. p = 20 units, a = 16 square units

**Shape Designs** ............................... **96**
Shapes will vary.

**Block Letters** ................................. **97**
Answers will vary.

**Graphing Words** ............................ **98**
Answers will vary.

**Outdoor Area** ................................ **99**
Answers will vary.

**What Are You Measuring?** ............. **100**
1. area
2. volume
3. distance

**Measuring Words** ........................... **101**
1. Surface area is the amount of space on the face of an object.
2. Volume is the amount of space an object holds.
3. Volume is greater.
4. Answers will vary.

**Create Your Own Problems** ........... **102–104**
Answers will vary.

**Check Your Skills** ......................... **105–108**
1. a
2. b
3. b
4. c
5. a
6. c
7. c
8. a
9. a
10. c
11. b
12. b
13. a

© Carson-Dellosa

0-7424-2893-1 • Using the Standards–Measurement 3

# Answer Key

**14.** b

**15.** b

**16.** c

**17.** a

**18.** b

**19.** b

**20.** b

**Post Test** ........................................109–110

  **1.** b

  **2.** b

  **3.** c

  **4.** b

  **5.** b

  **6.** b

  **7.** b

  **8.** c

  **9.** c

**10.** 16

**11.** b

**12.** b

© Carson-Dellosa

# Reproducible Rulers

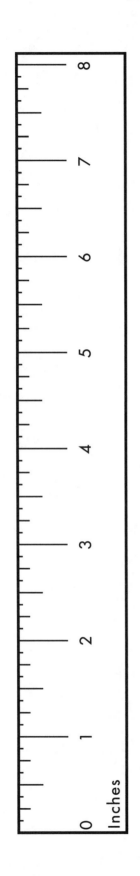

© Carson-Dellosa

| | |
|---|---|
| **inch**<br>**in.** | **foot**<br>**ft.** |
| **yard**<br>**yd.** | **mile**<br>**mi.** |
| **pound**<br>**lb.** | **ounce**<br>**oz.** |

© Carson-Dellosa

**customary unit of length**
(12 inches)

**customary measurement used to measure length**
(about the size of the top of your little finger)

**customary unit of length**
(5,280 feet)

**customary unit of length**

**customary unit of weight**
(used to measure smaller quantities)

**customary unit of weight**
(used to measure larger quantities)

© Carson-Dellosa

cup
c.

pint
pt.

quart
qt.

gallon
gal.

Fahrenheit
°F

Celsius
°C

© Carson-Dellosa

**customary unit of capacity**
(2 cups)

**customary unit of capacity**
(8 fluid ounces)

**customary unit of capacity**

**customary unit of capacity**
(4 cups)

**metric unit of temperature**
(water freezes at 0°;
water boils at 100°)

**customary unit of
temperature**
(water freezes at 32°;
water boils at 212°)

124

© Carson-Dellosa

| | |
|---|---|
| **centimeter**<br>**cm** | **meter**<br>**m** |
| **kilometer**<br>**km** | **gram**<br>**g** |
| **kilogram**<br>**kg** | **milliliter**<br>**mL** |

© Carson-Dellosa

**metric unit of length**
(100 cm)

**metric unit of length**
(2.5 cm = about 1 in.)

**metric unit of weight**
(used for small amounts)

**metric unit of length**
(1,000 m)

**metric unit of volume**
(used for small amounts)

**metric unit of weight**

© Carson-Dellosa

| liter L | volume |
|---------|--------|
| weight | area |
| length | temperature |

© Carson-Dellosa

0-7424-2893-1 • Using the Standards–Measurement 3

the amount a
container can hold

metric unit of volume
(1,000 mL)

the space that
an object covers

how heavy or light
something is

how hot or cold
something is

how long or short
something is

© Carson-Dellosa